The Philharmonic Society of London

From its Foundation, 1813, to its Fiftieth Year, 1862

GEORGE HOGARTH

CAMBRIDGE UNIVERSITY PRESS

Cambridge, New York, Melbourne, Madrid, Cape Town, Singapore,
São Paolo, Delhi, Dubai, Tokyo

Published in the United States of America by Cambridge University Press, New York

www.cambridge.org
Information on this title: www.cambridge.org/9781108001038

© in this compilation Cambridge University Press 2009

This edition first published 1862
This digitally printed version 2009

ISBN 978-1-108-00103-8 Paperback

This book reproduces the text of the original edition. The content and language reflect the beliefs, practices and terminology of their time, and have not been updated.

Cambridge University Press wishes to make clear that the book, unless originally published by Cambridge, is not being republished by, in association or collaboration with, or with the endorsement or approval of, the original publisher or its successors in title.

THE PHILHARMONIC SOCIETY

OF

LONDON;

FROM ITS FOUNDATION, 1813, TO ITS
FIFTIETH YEAR, 1862.

BY

GEORGE HOGARTH.

LONDON:
BRADBURY & EVANS, 11, BOUVERIE STREET, E.C., AND
ADDISON, HOLLIER, & LUCAS, 210, REGENT STREET.
1862.

PREFACE.

I HAVE been induced to write the following pages by the consideration that a brief Memoir of the Philharmonic Society of London, at the close of half-a-century of its existence, may excite interest among the lovers of an art, the advancement of which, not only in England but throughout the civilised world, has during this long period been so greatly promoted by its labours. And this interest, I venture to think, will be felt, in an especial measure, by the numerous body of musicians and amateurs, both in this and other countries, who have been more or less connected with the Society in various capacities; as subscribers to its concerts, as composers and performers whose talents it has called into action, and as members and associates of the Society itself. I cannot but think that a view of its career, obtained even from a narrative so simple and unpretending as mine, may prove instructive as well as pleasing, by showing the means whereby the Philharmonic Society has gained an extent of influence surpassing that of any similar institution, and, notwithstanding the competition of younger rivals, and the vast increase in the number of musical entertainments, has reached its "Jubilee Year" in the enjoyment of "a green old age," undecayed in vigour, resources, and means of usefulness.

THE

PHILHARMONIC SOCIETY.

THE Philharmonic Society of London was founded in the year 1813. It was projected by a small number of eminent professional musicians, with the view of promoting the cultivation of instrumental—and especially orchestral—music, which, in this country, had not received due attention, and was not in a condition corresponding to the generally advanced state of the Musical Art. The immortal symphonies of Haydn (some of them composed and first performed in London), those of Mozart, several of those of Beethoven, and a large body of the Quartets and other concerted instrumental music of the same great masters, had long been given to the world; but they were known to and appreciated only by musicians and amateurs (then a narrow circle), while they remained nearly a sealed book to the public, who were almost destitute of the means of hearing and acquiring a taste for them. Twenty years before, there was a promise of progress, when Haydn, brought expressly two several times from Vienna for that purpose, composed his twelve "Grand Symphonies" for Salomon's Concerts, and when they were performed in Hanover Square to applauding audiences. But the impulse to public taste given by that spirited *impresario* was not followed up, and Haydn's symphonies were heard no longer.

At the period when the Philharmonic Society was projected, there was not in London any orchestra formed for, and capable of, the performance of what is properly called orchestral music; — music, that is, intended to produce its effect wholly by the combination of instruments, independently of any connection with the voice. The band of the Italian Opera, and those of our musical theatres, such as they were in those days, are not to be taken into account; for their capabilities and their employment were limited to the slight overtures and meagre accompaniments of the Italian and English Operas then in vogue, German Opera being yet a stranger to our theatres.* The orchestra of the Ancient Concerts was fine and powerful; but the plan of those concerts excluded the orchestral works of the modern school. There only remained the orchestras (anything but select) got up at Drury Lane and Covent Garden Theatres for what were called the "Lent Oratorios,"—which have long since been abolished.

It was at this period of orchestral destitution (as we may call it) that the Philharmonic Society was established. The views of its founders are

* Mozart's *chef d'œuvre*, "Don Giovanni," was literally introduced to the English public through its splendid production by Mr. Ayrton in 1817.

clearly stated in their preliminary announcement.

"The want of encouragement," they say, "which has for many years past been experienced by that species of music which called forth the efforts, and displayed the genius of the greatest masters, and the almost utter neglect into which instrumental pieces in general have fallen, have long been sources of regret to the real amateur and to the well educated professor; a regret which, though it has hitherto proved unavailing, has not extinguished the hope that persevering exertions may yet restore to the world those compositions which have excited so much delight, and rekindle in the public mind that taste for excellence in instrumental music which has so long remained in a latent state. In order to effect this desirable purpose, several members of the musical profession have associated themselves, under the title of THE PHILHARMONIC SOCIETY, the object of which is to promote the performance, in the most perfect manner possible, of the best and most approved instrumental music, consisting of full pieces, concertantes for not less than three principal instruments, sestets, quintets, and trios; excluding concertos, solos, and duets; and requiring that vocal music, when introduced, shall have full orchestral accompaniments, and shall be subjected to the same restrictions."

These views have been adhered to during the whole career of the Society down to the present day, with only one deviation of any importance: concertos are no longer excluded. The concerto belongs in reality to the class of orchestral music, and an adherence to the original rules in this respect would have been at variance with their spirit.

Among the Rules adopted at the formation of the Society the following were the most important :—

> "The Society to consist of thirty Members, and an unlimited number of Associates, from whom all future Members shall be chosen. Members and Associates to pay an annual subscription of three guineas.
>
> "The subscription to the concerts, eight in number, to be

four guineas ; and for resident Members in the families of subscribers, two guineas each. No tickets to be transferable.

"Seven Directors to be annually chosen from among the Members, for the management of the concerts.

"No Member or Associate shall receive any emolument from the funds, all money received being appropriated only to the public purposes of the Society ; nor shall any Member or Associate receive any pecuniary recompense for assisting at the concerts.

"There shall not be any distinction of rank in the orchestra, and therefore the station of every performer shall be absolutely determined by the leader of the night."

The following are the names of the thirty Members who originally formed the Society :—

Messrs. Ashe.	Messrs. Griffin.
,, C. A. Ashley.	,, Hill.
,, Attwood.	,, Horsley.
,, Ayrton.	,, W. Knyvett.
,, Bartleman.	,, Moralt.
,, Berger.	,, Neate.
,, Bishop.	,, Novello.
,, Blake.	,, R. Potter.
,, Clementi.	,, Salomon.
,, R. Cooke.	,, Sherrington.
,, P. A. Corri.	,, Shield.
,, Cramer.	,, Sir G. Smart.
,, F. Cramer.	,, Viotti.
,, Dance.	,, S. Webbe, Jun.
,, Graeff.	,, Yaniewicz.

THE PHILHARMONIC SOCIETY. 7

The following were the twenty-five original Associates :—

Messrs. Beale.	Messrs. Meves.
,, Bomtempo.	,, P. Meyer.
,, Brugier	,, C. Meyer.
,, Burrowes.	,, Mori.
,, Cudmore.	,, Naldi.
,, H. Gattie.	,, Peile.
,, Hawes.	,, T. Rawlins.
,, C. Horn.	,, Saffery.
,, Hunter.	,, C. Smith.
,, Kellner.	,, Spagnoletti.
,, Kramer.	,, Vaccari.
,, Latour.	,, Welsh.
,, Lord.	

In these lists the musical reader will find the well-remembered names of many of the most eminent musicians of the time.

The Directors for the first season were Messrs. Ayrton, Bishop, Clementi, P. A. Corri, J. B. Cramer, F. Cramer, and Dance.

The Orchestra, as originally constituted, included the most eminent instrumentalists then resident in London. The performances were conducted in a different manner from the present. For each concert two individuals were appointed by the Directors ; the one to occupy the place of principal violin, with the title of "Leader of the Orchestra," and the other to "preside at the pianoforte." The duty of the leader was not only to execute his own part with exemplary accuracy and firmness, but to attend to all the other performers, who were to look to him for the time of the movements, and to be governed by his beat. His coadjutor, at the pianoforte, and with the full score before him, was to watch the performance and to be ready to correct any mistake. This method, borrowed from the usages (far from uniform) of foreign theatrical and other orchestras, was liable to obvious objections. Neither of these functionaries could efficiently perform his duties separately, and they could not perform them jointly without interfering and clashing with each other. The leader could not execute his own part properly, and at the same time attend to, and beat time to, the whole band ; while the person at the pianoforte could scarcely exercise any influence on the " going " of the performance without coming into collision with the leader. At rehearsals he could be of much use, but of none at concerts. In practice, however, this anomalous kind of double rule gradually corrected itself. It was found that the individual who "presided at the pianoforte" with the score before him, and his undivided attention given to the orchestra, was in the best condition to control its movements. He, accordingly, became the real conductor, while the title of leader became merely nominal; until at length even the title was abolished, and the Philharmonic as well as every other great orchestra is now a monarchy, under the sway of that powerful sovereign, the CONDUCTOR. How these successive changes took place in the constitution of the Philharmonic Band we shall point out as we proceed.

The concerts were originally given at the Argyll Rooms, then recently built; a spacious and elegant structure, which was unfortunately destroyed by fire in the year 1830.

The first concert took place on the 8th of March, 1813. The following was the programme, which we quote at length, as illustrating the views originally entertained as to the plan and arrangement of the concerts:—

PART I.

Overture to Anacreon . . .	CHERUBINI.
Quartetto—two violins, viola, and violoncello. Messrs. F. Cramer, Moralt, Sherrington, and Lindley . . .	MOZART.
Quartetto and Chorus, "Nell' Orror." Mrs. Moralt, Messrs. Hawes, P. A. Corri, and Kellner . . .	SACCHINI.
Serenade—wind instruments. Messrs. Mahon, Oliver, Holmes, Tully, and the Petrides	MOZART.
Symphony	BEETHOVEN.

PART II.

Symphony	HAYDN.
Chorus, "Placido è il Mar." Mrs. Moralt, Miss Hughes, Messrs. P. A. Corri, C. Smith, &c. . . .	MOZART.
Quintetto—two violins, viola, and two violoncellos. Messrs. Salomon, Cudmore, Sherrington, Lindley, and C. Ashley	BOCCHERINI.
Chaconne, Jomelli, and March . .	HAYDN.

Leader, MR. SALOMON. Pianoforte, MR. CLEMENTI.

At this concert, it will be observed, the vocal music consisted only of concerted pieces. Though there was no express prohibition of solos, they were practically excluded for several seasons. The first air introduced into a Philharmonic Concert was Mozart's "Dove Sono," sung by Miss Stephens on March 25, 1816.

Quartets, quintets, and other concerted pieces for solo instruments, without the orchestra, were originally considered an essential feature of the concerts, and continued in constant use for many years. Formerly this description of music could not otherwise be heard in public. But when "Classical Chamber Concerts" came to be established by various parties of our first-rate instrumentalists, and to be frequented by amateurs, it was no longer necessary to introduce such pieces into the Philharmonic Concerts, and latterly they have been discontinued; those concerted pieces only being still introduced which demand the orchestra, or require too many performers to be classed under the denomination of chamber music.

During the first season the leaders of the various concerts were Mr. Salomon, Mr. F. Cramer, Mr. Spagnoletti, Mr. Viotti, Mr. Yaniewicz, and Mr. Vaccari. Mr. Clementi and Mr. Cramer presided at the pianoforte.

The concerts of the first season present little more that calls for remark. Boccherini, whose name appears in the above programme, was one of the most celebrated instrumental composers of the last century. His quintets are esteemed his best work, being remarkable for their grace, refinement, and pure Italian style. Viotti, it is said, used to play them in preference to any other chamber music. They have been unable, however, to contend with the superior strength and energy of the modern German school, and have, though undeservedly, almost fallen into oblivion. At another concert of this season there was a symphony by another once famed but now forgotten composer, Pleyel, once the most popular symphonist of his day, and able to divide the palm even with Haydn and Mozart. The other symphonies performed during the season were by Haydn, Mozart, Beethoven, Clementi, Andreas Romberg, and Woelfl. Unfortunately the early programmes are slightly drawn up, and do not specify the particular symphonies of the great masters that were produced; but we see that the works of Beethoven had not at first the preponderance that they afterwards obtained. In the season of 1813 there were three symphonies of this composer; in 1814, two; and in 1815, two. At this period Beethoven's first six symphonies only had been given to the world.

At the first concert of the season, 1814, a manuscript symphony, composed by Ferdinand Ries expressly for the Society, was performed for the first time. This composer's fame has not been so durable as it at first promised to be. He was a great pianist, and his voluminous works have every good quality, save that of originality, the only quality which confers permanent vitality. At the second concert there was a quartet for two violins, viola, and violoncello, by the now veteran Griffin, one of the few surviving founders of the Society. Mr. Griffin early distinguished himself by several works of great merit, but (as has been the case with many English musicians) his attention was diverted from composition to the labours of what is in this country a more advantageous branch of his profession. At the seventh concert there was a manuscript symphony by Dr. Crotch, the celebrated author of "Palestine," then a member of the Society.

The season of 1815 was rendered memorable by the arrival of the illustrious Cherubini in England. At the third concert he conducted in person the performance of his own overture to *Anacreon*, and was received with the honour due to so great a master. At the subsequent concert he conducted the performance of a manuscript overture, composed by him expressly for the Society. On the 12th of June he was elected an Associate, and, on the 19th of the same month, a Member of the Society. At the seventh concert of this season a quintet, by Mr. J. B. Cramer, for the pianoforte and stringed instruments, was performed by the composer, with Messrs. F. Cramer, Moralt, Lindley, and Hill. At the eighth concert there was a new overture by Cherubini, which had been previously performed at his own concert; and at the same concert the celebrated violinist, Lafont, made his first appearance in a "Sinfonia Concertante" composed by himself.

In the season of 1816, the Parisian violinist, Baillot (who visited England for the first time), took a large share in the performances. At the first concert he performed a concertante of his own, and a quartet of Mozart; and at the sixth and seventh, besides joining in concerted pieces, he acted as leader. Baillot was a great performer: his quartet-playing, especially, was regarded as a model of classical purity. At the second concert a manuscript overture, by Mr. Cipriani Potter, was performed; the first of a series of masterly works which Mr. Potter has composed for the Society. At the fifth concert, a septet for the pianoforte and stringed instruments, by Mr. Potter, was performed for the first time, the principal part being played by himself. At this concert a manuscript motet, "Father of Light," by Mr. Samuel Wesley, was performed, the solo parts sung by Mrs. Salmon, Mr. Goss, Mr. Braham, and Mr. C. Smith. And likewise, at this very interesting concert, there was a new cantata, "La Primavera," by Cherubini, composed expressly for the Society. At the eighth concert, M. Kalkbrenner performed the principal part of a pianoforte concertante composed by himself.

In the course of this season Mr. Weichsell, Mr. Mori, and Mr. Baillot acted for the first time as leaders of the orchestra, and Sir George Smart presided for the first time at the pianoforte.

The season 1817 presents several particulars worthy of being recorded.—At the first concert Beethoven's overture to *Fidelio* was performed for the first time in this country. At the second, Mr. Potter played the principal part of a pianoforte quartet of Dussek, a composer whose admirable works, especially for this instrument, have for a long time been too much neglected. At the fourth concert, Mr. Griffin's pianoforte quartet was repeated, the principal part being played by him. In a concertante for the Spanish guitar, composed and performed by M. Sor, a guitarist in great vogue at that time, he astonished the audience by his unrivalled execution. At the seventh concert, Beethoven's "Adelaida," then new to the English public, was sung by Miss Goodall (a young singer then rising into great favour, but who retired early from the profession) and accompanied on the pianoforte by Sir George Smart. This concert opened with a manuscript symphony, composed and presented to the Society by Lord Burghersh, the late Earl of Westmoreland. At the same concert Beethoven's seventh symphony in A, which had then newly appeared in Germany, was performed for the first time ; the Directors having, in order to its production, procured copies from Germany.

It appears from the minutes of a General Meeting on the 11th of July, 1815, that Beethoven having, through the medium of Mr. Neate, made an offer to the Society of three manuscript overtures for seventy-five guineas, the purchase at that price was agreed to. In 1817 some correspondence took place with Beethoven respecting his paying a visit to England. An offer was made to him of three hundred guineas in consideration of his coming to London and superintending the production of two symphonies to be composed by him for the Society. In answer he demanded four hundred guineas, one hundred and fifty to be paid in advance. It appears from a minute of the Directors in August, 1817, that the previous offer was then repeated, but the arrangement was not carried into effect, Beethoven having ultimately abandoned the intention which he at one time entertained of visiting this country.

A new system of musical tuition, introduced into this country by M. Logier, excited great attention in the musical world at this period. It was specially applied to teaching the pianoforte, and the principles of harmony or thorough bass, and its principal peculiarity was, that these branches were taught in classes. A treatise on the system was published by M. Logier in London, and, by means of exhibitions of this gentleman's pupils, got up in London and in all parts of the kingdom, by himself and his assistants, his method gained very great popularity. In every considerable town Logierian Academies sprang up, in which a dozen or twenty pianos, under the fingers often of twice the number of young ladies, kept up an incessant discord, to the edification of delighted mammas, who each thought that her own darling was the chief performer in the concert, and who were moreover tempted by the comparatively cheap rate at which the power of doing such wonders was imparted. The subject at the same time gave rise to much controversy ; pamphlets on both sides appeared in London, in Edinburgh, in Dublin, and in Glasgow, and a paper war raged throughout the land. We find, from the records of the Philharmonic Society, that it was involved in the dispute. One of M. Logier's exhibitions was attended, among a number of musical people, by several eminent members of the Society; and a newspaper article appeared, avowedly proceeding from M. Logier himself, in which the alleged approbation of those members was represented as a testimony of the Society to the merits of the system. The matter having been brought before a general meeting on the 20th of November, 1817, the following statement, by order of that meeting, was published in the principal journals :—

"A report being in circulation that this Society has examined into, and approved of, a new system of musical education, it is judged expedient to apprise the public that, although several members of this body did attend an exhibition of some pupils instructed by a new method, and that, though they were pleased with the alacrity and diligent attention of the pupils, and manifested that feeling by the usual mode of applause, yet they in no way expressed their approbation of any part of the system that claims the merit of originality. On the contrary, they almost unanimously agreed in an opinion by no means favourable to either the principle or practice of the novel mode of instruction now attempted to be introduced."

Some further controversy took place, of a personal nature, which it is unnecessary to revive, it being sufficient to record the early and decided opinion given by the Philharmonic Society respecting a system which, though for a time it did much mischief, has long since disappeared as one of the exploded bubbles of the day. An able and conclusive pamphlet, drawn up by a committee of the principal professors of music in London, contributed to this result; and though "Logierian Academies" continued to be carried on, both in London and the provinces, for a good many years after Logier himself had left the country, not one, we believe, now exists.

In the season of 1818, the only remarkable novelty was Hummel's septet in D minor, for the pianoforte, with wind and stringed instruments, which was produced at the first concert, the principal part performed by Mr. Neate. During this and the following season, a considerable sensation was made by the appearance of the Demoiselles De Lihu, two young French ladies, whose elegant and finished duet-singing had deservedly gained great favour on the Continent.

In 1819 the programmes began to be more fully drawn up, and to contain the words of the vocal pieces. At the second concert a pianoforte quintet, composed by Mr. Ries for these concerts, was performed by him for the first time. At the fourth concert Beethoven's dramatic scena, "Ah perfido!" was sung by Mr. Braham, under the title of " Ah Perfid*a*," changing the voice from a soprano to a tenor, and the subject from the passionate complaint of the forsaken Medea to that of some nameless *inamorato*, whining for the loss of his mistress.

This scene demands a female tragedian of the highest vocal powers; and though other tenors have taken the unwarrantable liberty of which Mr. Braham set the example, it will not probably be now repeated. At the seventh concert there was a stringed-instrument quartet by Griffin, and a manuscript Italian terzetto, *La Solitudine*, composed by Attwood, and sung by Messrs. Welsh, Braham, and Sale.

The year 1820 was memorable as being the period of Spohr's first arrival in England. At the first concert of this season he performed his concerto, *Nello Stilo Drammatico*, a work now well known to the musical public. At the fourth concert a duet for the violin and harp was played by M. and Madame Spohr,—his first wife, an accomplished and interesting lady, and a finished performer on her instrument. At the sixth concert he played (with Messrs. Watts, Mountain, and Lindley), one of his own quartets; and at the eighth, his new symphony was performed for the first time, together with his nonetto for stringed and wind instruments, in which he sustained the principal part.* At the general meeting on the 1st of July, a message

---

* On the evening after this Philharmonic Concert, Spohr's benefit concert took place. It was attended with remarkable circumstances, of which, in his "Autobiography," published since his death, he gives an affecting account. "My concert," he says, "took place on the 20th of June, the day on which Queen Charlotte [Caroline] returned from Italy, and made her entry into London, in order to appear before Parliament on the accusation of adultery. All London was split into two parties: the most numerous, which consisted of the middle classes and the rabble, declared loudly in favour of the Queen. The town was in the most violent agitation. The programmes of my concert, posted at the street-corners, had disappeared under immense placards, ordering, in the name of the people, a general illumination of the city. My servant came to tell me that the mob were going to break every window that was not illuminated. My wife, who, moreover, was anxious about her appearance at the concert, began to tremble with fear of the dangers which threatened. I endeavoured to re-assure her as well as I could, and succeeded. My new symphony was magnificently executed, and had even greater success than on its first performance. During the air which followed, 'Revenge, Timotheus cries,' of Handel, I tuned my wife's harp in the antechamber, and led her into the room. Our duet was about to begin; the audience were all attention, and listened in silence to our first chords, when suddenly a frightful uproar was heard in the street, followed by volleys of stones against the unilluminated windows of the adjoining house. They were lit up immediately, and the multitude went their way with loud huzzas. The company resumed

was delivered from M. Spohr, requesting permission to dedicate his new symphony to the Society — a compliment from the illustrious composer which was duly acknowledged. His residence in London at this time, and the just homage paid to his genius, laid the foundation of that intercourse between him and the English public which lasted to the end of his life, and was productive of vast benefits to the art in this country. He had not as yet begun his career in the highest of its branches, the oratorio, nor produced any of those master-works of this class on which his most durable fame will rest —works, for the existence of which the world is unquestionably indebted to his sojourn here; for it was here that his attention was especially

their places, and, when quiet was restored, we recommenced our piece. I dreaded the effect of the alarm on Dorette's playing, and anxiously listened to her first chords, which were full and vigorous. Our success went on increasing to the conclusion of the duet, and when we concluded, I thought the applause would never come to an end. When, delighted with our triumph, we came down from the orchestra elated and happy, we little thought that Dorette had touched the harp for the last time!"

called to, and his genius stimulated by, the oratorios of Handel. A few years later, we may add, the same cause produced the same effect, in influencing the career of Mendelssohn. But Spohr, when he first came to England, was in the zenith of his reputation, as the greatest violinist of the age, and unrivalled for that classic purity of style and finish of execution which the most gifted of his successors have not to this day been able to surpass. As an instrumental composer his name stood lower only than the three great names which must ever be united—Haydn, Mozart, and Beethoven; and, in vocal music he had already begun his splendid contributions to the German Opera stage—Spohr's arrival in London, in short, was a great event in the annals of music in this country.

In this year, 1820, the individual who presided at the pianoforte was, for the first time, in the programmes denominated "Conductor." And, in the following year, the pianoforte was removed, and the conductor stationed, as at present, in a desk in front of the orchestra. The title of leader, nevertheless, was still bestowed upon the principal violin; and this continued to be the case till the appointment of Mr. Costa to the office of conductor in the year 1846; though long before that time the title of leader had become merely nominal.

The season of 1821 was distinguished by the first appearances of the celebrated violinist Kiesewetter; of Tolou, then esteemed the most marvellous flute-player in Europe; and of a still more important person than either, "Mr. Moscheles of Vienna," who performed a manuscript concerto of his own at the eighth concert on the 11th of June. No first appearance of an instrumental performer ever created a greater sensation than this. Moscheles at that time was the greatest *bravura* performer that had ever been heard. His powers of execution excited as much surprise as those of Thalberg did at a later period; while his music, calculated for the fullest display of those powers, possessed a vigorous invention, and the solid and masterly style derived from the profoundest study of his art. This appearance at a Philharmonic Concert was the commencement of a brilliant career of a quarter of a century, passed wholly in England, and terminated by his acceptance, in 1846, of a position combining honour with comparative ease, a Professor's chair in the Conservatoire of Leipzig, which he still holds, to the great advantage of that distinguished school of music.*

At the second concert of this season Mozart's pianoforte concerto in D was played, for the first time in this country, and with great effect, by Mr. Potter; and a new manuscript

* Moscheles, during a visit to London last year, was prevailed upon to appear once more at a Philharmonic Concert. On the 24th of June, 1861, at the last concert of the season, he performed his concerto in G minor to an overflowing assemblage; exhibiting the fire and energy of his prime, filling his older listeners with pleasing reminiscences of their early days, and convincing the younger portion of the audience that the illustrious veteran, of whom they had heard so much, was well worthy of his fame.

overture, composed by Spohr expressly for the Society, was performed at the same concert.

The season of 1822 was remarkable, among other things, for the production of a new concerto for the pianoforte, "with characteristic rondo *and chorus*," composed by Steibelt, the pianoforte part performed by Mr. Neate. This union of choral with instrumental music was at that time a novelty. From the words of the chorus, the subject of the piece seems to have been gay and joyous, and the music, though it is now forgotten, we may suppose, from the character of the composer, to have been brilliant and effective. Steibelt's success was confined to pianoforte music; and some of his works for that instrument, as well as those of Dussek, Woelfl, &c., deserve to be rescued from oblivion. This season was also remarkable for Mrs. Anderson's first appearance at these concerts. Her performance on the 29th of April, 1822, of Hummel's concerto in B minor, was the commencement of a career not surpassed in brilliancy by that of any female pianist in Europe.

The new works produced in the years 1823 and 1824 were a pianoforte fantasia, with orchestral accompaniments, by Czerny, performed by Mr. Neate; a manuscript overture composed for the Society by Cherubini; Beethoven's pianoforte concerto in C minor, performed for the first time in this country by Mr. Potter; a new manuscript overture by Mr. Clementi, and a new concerto composed and performed by Mr. Kalkbrenner.

The name of Weber began to be known in this country by the production of the *Freischütz* in 1824, first at the English Opera-house and then at the two great theatres, in various versions, and with alterations and mutilations which would not be tolerated now-a-days, but, nevertheless, with a degree of success almost without example. At the first concert of the season, 1825, the overture to *Euryanthe* was performed, this being the first time of any of Weber's compositions being heard at these concerts. In the course of the season a number of his pieces, both vocal and instrumental, were brought forward, particularly his orchestral *chef d'œuvre*, the overture to the *Freischütz*, the famous scena from the opera, "Before my eyes beheld him," sung with great brilliancy by Miss Stephens, and a pianoforte concerto performed in a masterly manner by Mr. Neate.

In this season Beethoven's famous ninth or choral symphony was performed for the first time in England. This memorable occurrence took place on the 21st of March, 1825. The symphony occupied the second act of the concert, and is thus designated in the programme: "New Grand Characteristic Sinfonia, MS. with vocal finale, the principal parts to be sung by Madame Caradori, Miss Goodall, Mr. Vaughan, and Mr. Phillips ; *composed expressly for this Society.*" The performance was conducted by Sir George Smart.

The composition of this symphony was the result of a meeting of the Directors on the 10th of November, 1822, at which it was resolved to offer Beethoven fifty pounds for a MS. symphony, it being stipulated that it should be delivered during the month of March following, and that the composer should be at liberty to dispose of it at the expiration of eighteen months after its receipt. The money was immediately advanced, but the symphony was not received till long past the stipulated time—not, indeed, till after it had been performed at Vienna, at a great concert on the 7th of May, 1824, got up by the aristocracy of that city for the benefit of the composer, on which occasion Beethoven made his last appearance in public. The remuneration, therefore, received by him from the Philharmonic Society was not only adequate but ample, considering that the symphony had not only been performed, but published in score at Vienna, before the Society had it in their power to make any use of it.

Its first performance in London was not very successful. A work so new and strange, not only in its design and construction, but in its most minute details, and so full of difficulties for the performers, was but imperfectly understood either by the orchestra or the audience. The account of the concert in "The Harmonicon," well known to be from the pen of a most distinguished critic, himself a member of the Society, contains the following remarks, which show the impression made by this performance, even on the most enlightened portion of the public :—" In the present symphony we discover no diminution of Beethoven's creative talent; it exhibits many perfectly new traits, and in its technical formation shows amazing ingenuity and unabated vigour of mind. But, with all the merits that it unquestionably possesses, it is at least twice as long as it should be; it repeats itself, and the subjects in consequence become weak by reiteration. The last movement, a chorus, is heterogeneous; and though there is much vocal beauty in parts of it, yet it does not, and no habit will ever make it mix up with the first three movements. This chorus is a hymn to

Joy, commencing with a recitative and relieved by many *soli* passages. What relation it bears to the symphony we could not make out; and here, as well as in other parts, the want of intelligible design is too apparent."* This first

* It is no part of my design, in this little narrative, to enter into disputed questions of musical criticism. The general opinion of the musical world, in regard to the merits of this symphony, is greatly changed since the period of which I am now speaking. But it is not surprising that such criticisms as the above should have been made at that period when it is considered that opinions precisely similar continue to be held, *even now*, by musicians of the highest authority. In Spohr's posthumous "Autobiography," recently published in Germany, there are the following remarks on Beethoven's latest works, including the symphony in question:—" Up to this point in his musical career" (the production of the seventh symphony) "there was no perceptible decay in the creative power of Beethoven's genius. But as his growing deafness no longer allowed him to hear any music, his infirmity must necessarily have had an injurious influence on his imagination. His continual efforts to be original and to follow a new path, could not be unaccompanied by error, now that his faculties were unaided by the corrective sense of hearing. Was it, then, matter of surprise that his compositions became more and more obscure, unintelligible, and incoherent? There are persons, indeed, who think they understand these later productions, and, in their joy over the supposed discovery, place them far above the earlier masterpieces. I am not, however, one of those ; and, for my own part, frankly con-

attempt to produce Beethoven's colossal work was not encouraging. The conductor, Sir George Smart, with laudable modesty, felt doubts as to his own correctness in giving the times of the different movements; and having occasion, during the same season, to visit Dresden, in order to make arrangements for the production of *Oberon* at Covent Garden, extended his journey to Vienna for the express purpose of obtaining information respecting the performance of the ninth symphony from personal communication with Beethoven himself—a characteristic trait of

fess that I could never prevail upon myself to like the latest works of Beethoven. Indeed, the much-admired ninth symphony I am compelled to place in this category. The first three movements of this work, in spite of occasional flashes of genius, I consider much inferior to those in the eight preceding symphonies, while the fourth movement seems to me so monstrous, so devoid of taste, so trivial in the setting of Schiller's ode, that I have never been able to understand how a genius like Beethoven's could ever fall so low. Were there no others, this instance is sufficient to confirm the correctness of the opinion I had already formed in Vienna, that Beethoven was wanting in æsthetic culture and in the sense of the beautiful."

zeal and energy. No further attempt, however, was made to reproduce this arduous work for no less a period than twelve years, till 1837, when it was performed a second time under better auspices.

Weber came to London in 1826; and, as might be expected, his visit was a remarkable event in the annals of the Philharmonic Society. The special purpose of his visit was to superintend the production of his *Oberon* at Covent Garden Theatre, which, under the management of Mr. Charles Kemble, and under the musical direction of Sir George Smart, was then an "English Opera-house." Weber had engaged, two years before, to compose this opera, the drama of which (a very beautiful poem) was written for him by Mr. Planché; and the arrangements for its production, and for the composer's visit to London were made in the course of a visit paid to him at Dresden, during the previous season, by Mr. Kemble and Sir George Smart. Weber arrived in London in the beginning of March, and took up his residence under Sir

George's hospitable roof. *Oberon* was immediately put in rehearsal, and Weber, in one of his charming letters written from London to his wife, spoke of the theatre and the company in a spirit of candour and liberality not always exhibited by foreign celebrities who visit our shores. " I can assure you," he said, " that you may be quite at ease both as to the singers and the orchestra. Miss Paton is a singer of the first rank, and will play Reiza divinely. Braham not less so, though in a totally different style. There are also several good tenors, and I really cannot see why the English singing should be so much abused. The singers have a perfectly good Italian education, fine voices, and expression. The orchestra is not remarkable, but still very good, and the chorus particularly so. In short, I feel quite at ease as to the fate of *Oberon.*" The opera was produced on the 12th of April ; and the account of its reception must be given in Weber's own most touching words. " My best beloved Caroline," he wrote, " through God's grace and assistance I have this evening met with the most complete success. The brilliancy and affecting nature of the triumph is indescribable. God alone be thanked for it! When I entered the orchestra, the whole of the house, which was filled to overflowing, rose up, and I was saluted by huzzas and waving of hats and handkerchiefs, which I thought would never have done. They insisted on encoring the overture. Every air was interrupted twice or thrice with bursts of applause." And he concluded : " So much for this night, dear life, from your heartily tired husband, who cannot sleep in peace till he has communicated to you this new blessing."

While *Oberon* was still in preparation, Weber was requested by the directors of the Philharmonic Society to conduct one of the concerts. He accordingly conducted the third concert of the season, on the 3rd of April; and this was his first public appearance in London. It excited intense interest, and the room was filled to the doors with a brilliant assembly, composed of persons distinguished not only in music, but in art, literature, and fashion. His reception was enthusiastic; and he showed, by expressive gestures, the gratitude and pleasure with which he received so strong a manifestation of feeling. The programme included four pieces by him: The great tenor scena from the *Freischütz* sung by Mr. Sapio; the overture to *Euryanthe;* an Italian scena, " La dolce speranza," sung by Madame Caradori Allan; and the overture to the *Freischütz*. The rest of the concert consisted of Andreas Romberg's Symphony in E flat; Haydn's duet, " Graceful Consort," from *The Creation*, sung by Madame Caradori Allan and Mr. Phillips; a solo on the pianoforte by M. Schunke, an excellent performer; Beethoven's Symphony in A; a quartet of Haydn; and a vocal trio from *Don Giovanni*. Weber's clear and graceful manner of conducting was generally remarked.

When he arrived in London he was far gone in the fatal pulmonary disease under which he had long laboured, and which was aggravated by the unaccustomed severity of our English climate. On the morning of the 5th of June he was found dead in his bed in the house of Sir George Smart. He was cut off at the early age of forty, and (as his latest work showed) in the full strength and vigour of his mind; but it appeared, from the medical examination which took place after his death, that his life, under the most favourable circumstances, could have endured but a short time longer. The last Philharmonic concert of the season, on the 12th of June, commenced with Handel's Dead March in *Saul*, performed (in the words of the programme) " as a tribute to departed genius : " and on the 21st of that month his remains were interred in the vaults beneath .the Roman Catholic Chapel in Moorfields. The procession consisted of a numerous body, his friends and professional brethren, Sir George Smart being the chief mourner ; and the funeral service, in which the *Requiem* of Mozart was performed by a large vocal and instrumental band, took place in the presence of an assemblage of two thousand persons, who seemed deeply impressed by the solemnity of the occasion. Though this great artist, during his brief sojourn among us —his last on earth—mingled little in general society, and scarcely at all in the fashionable world, for intercourse with which he was not fitted by character or habits, yet his strong and cultivated intellect, simple manners, and genial spirit, gained the affection of many friends in this country, by whom his untimely death was deeply lamented.

The following year was marked by the death of a musician of a still higher order.

Beethoven died at Vienna on the 26th of March, 1827, after an illness of several months' duration, attended with dreadful sufferings — sufferings aggravated by the fear of impending destitution which haunted his mind. Under the influence of this feeling he applied, through the medium of his friend Mr. Stumpff, the harp manufacturer in Great Portland Street (a gentleman well known for his musical enthusiasm), and Mr. Moscheles, to the Philharmonic Society, requesting the society to give a concert for his benefit. A special general meeting, for the consideration of this request, was held on the 28th of February; and it was unanimously resolved, " that the sum of one hundred pounds be sent, through the hands of Mr. Moscheles, to some confidential friend of Beethoven, to be applied to his comforts and necessities during his illness." The money was instantly remitted; and its receipt was acknowledged by Beethoven himself, in the following interesting letter, addressed to Mr. Moscheles, and dated the 18th day of March, eight days before the death of the writer :—

"MY DEAR, GOOD MOSCHELES,

" With what feelings I read your letter of the 1st of March, I cannot find words to express. The generosity with which the Philharmonic Society have exceeded my request, has moved me to my inmost soul. I request you, my dear Moscheles, to be the organ by which I convey to the Philharmonic Society my heartfelt thanks for their kind sympathy and distinguished liberality. With regard to the concert which the Society intend to arrange for my benefit, I trust they will not relinquish that noble design, and beg that they will deduct the hundred pounds, which they have already sent me, from the profits. Should any surplus be left, and the Society be kindly willing to bestow it upon me, I hope to have it in my power to show my gratitude by composing for them either a new symphony, which already lies sketched on my desk, or a new overture, or anything else that the Society may prefer. Should Heaven only be pleased to restore me again to health, I will prove to the noble English how much I value their sympathy in my melancholy fate. Your noble conduct, my dear friend, will ever remain in my remembrances. I hope shortly to return my thanks to Sir George Smart and Mr. Stumpff. Farewell!"

Beethoven's spirits were greatly revived by the arrival of the Society's remittance. He said cheerfully to his friends about him, "Now we may again treat ourselves occasionally to a merry day," and desired to indulge in the luxury of a dish of fish that he was fond of. But, though the illustrious musician died in circumstances of neglect and penury, which will ever reflect disgrace upon his country, and especially of the great and wealthy capital in which he had spent almost the whole of his life, yet he was not in the state of absolute want which he had morbidly imagined. When the inventory of his effects came to be taken after his death, there were found, among some papers in an old decayed chest, Austrian bank bills to the value of about a thousand pounds in English money, with some hundred florins in paper money, besides the one hundred pounds sent by the Philharmonic Society, which remained untouched. This discovery made no small noise in Vienna; and the public were, or affected to be, much hurt at Beethoven's having applied for assistance of which he did not stand in need, and, what was worse, having applied to strangers in London instead of his friends and admirers in Vienna, by whom every necessary aid would have been promptly bestowed. But such clamours were idle and ridiculous. Beethoven, if not absolutely penniless, was miserably poor. It was well known to his "illustrious patrons" and his "numerous friends and admirers" that he had for years been living in penury and denying himself the common comforts of life. And what, after all, did the accumulated savings of this life of poverty and privation amount to? The magnificent sum of eleven or twelve hundred pounds sterling, yielding the ample revenue of thirty or forty pounds a year! No wonder that Beethoven, only turned of fifty, with the probability of many years of life, and yet disabled from labour, looked with dread upon the prospect of destitution: he might have done so even if his mind had not been enfeebled by disease. As to his applying to foreigners in London in preference to his friends and countrymen in Vienna, his doing so only showed the estimate he had been taught, by sad and lifelong experience, to form of the value of their friendship.

The concerts of the years 1827 and 1828 do not present many memorable incidents. The instrumental pieces performed for the first time during that period were, a concerto of Hummel performed by M. Schlesinger, a pupil of Ries and a pianist of distinguished excellence; a MS. violin concerto of Maurer, performed by Mr. Kiesewetter; a duet concertante for two violoncellos, of Bernard Romberg, played by Messrs. Lindley, father and son; a pianoforte fantasia of Weber, played by Mr. Neate; a

MS. flute concerto composed and played by the late Mr. Nicholson; a concertino of De Beriot, performed by himself, and MS. overtures by Mr. J. H. Griesbach and Mr. Goss, both of which were warmly received.* At the third concert of 1827, Mrs. Anderson performed Hummel's septuor in D minor with such remarkable effect, that she received the formal thanks of the Directors. The most favourite vocal performers were Miss Paton, Miss Stephens, Madame Caradori Allan, Madame Stockhausen, Miss Childe (afterwards Mrs. Seguin), Miss Bacon, Mrs. Braham, Signor Sapio, Signor Zuchelli, Sig. Curioni, Mr. Phillips, Signor Galli, M. Begrez, and Signor Pellegrini. Moreover, on the 21st of May, 1827, Liszt made his first appearance in a concerto of Hummel.

In the year 1827, at the general meeting of October 30th, a law was enacted which gave

* We find in "The Harmonicon" the following remarks on Mr. Goss's overture: "This composition, which does honour to the English school, is in F minor, is full of the most undeniable proofs of the author's skill, and shows that his genius wants nothing but encouragement."

rise to a good deal of discussion at the time. It was to the following effect: "Within three months after the death of any member, there shall be transferred to his legal personal representatives so much of the Society's stock in the public funds then standing in the names of the trustees as shall be equal to one share, the whole being divided into as many shares as there shall have been members living on the day before such death shall happen." This law, after much opposition, was passed by a majority of fifteen votes against six. It remained in force till the general meeting of the 22nd of November, 1830, when it was rescinded by a majority of twelve votes against one. It may be presumed that no such proposition as this will ever be brought forward again. The supposition that the members of a society like the Philharmonic have, as individuals, any right, in a commercial point of view, to the fund created by the excess of the yearly receipts above the expenditure, proceeds from an erroneous notion of the nature of that fund. The fund arises from money paid by the public to the Society for a specific purpose—that purpose being the provision of a certain musical entertainment. No subscriber to the concerts expects for a moment that any portion of the money paid by him will go into the pockets of members of the Society, to be used by them for their private purposes. The Society is a body of artists having no other than artistic objects. The concerts are carried on for the improvement and benefit of music in this country, without any view to pecuniary profit. The Society, then, having received from the public money for *one* purpose, has no right to convert it to *another*. When it happens that the sum received in any year exceeds the necessary expenditure of that year, the money remaining does not change its character. It still continues to be, what it was at first, money placed in the hands of the Society for a special artistic purpose; and it is still incumbent on the Society to apply it to that purpose whenever it shall be necessary.

It is obviously of great importance that such a fund should exist: it is a reserve to meet casualties and deficiencies; it is a protection against the fluctuations of seasons and the vicissitudes of events; and is therefore essential to the strength and stability of the Society. But it must be held under the obligation of being available, whenever requisite, for the artistic objects of the Society; and cannot be regarded as the property of the Members, or divisible among them individually.*

The first concert of the year 1828 was conducted by Mr. Clementi. This was the venerable musician's last appearance in public, and he was received by the audience with every mark of respect and esteem. He was then in his seventy-sixth year, having been born in 1752. He came to England at an early age, and, having entered into commerce, and become

---

* It is an express article of the Society's constitution, that "No Member or Associate shall receive any emolument from the funds, *all money received being appropriated only to the public purposes of the Society.*"

the head of the great house in Cheapside, which still exists, he passed nearly the whole of his long life in this country, where almost all his numerous works were given to the world. He died on the 10th of March, 1832, at the age of eighty.

Mendelssohn arrived in England for the first time in the spring of the year 1829. He was only in his twentieth year, but already not unknown to fame, and the reputation of his youthful genius had preceded him to this country. He was warmly welcomed by our most eminent musicians and amateurs, and his symphony in C minor, which he had brought with him, was performed at the seventh Philharmonic Concert on the 25th of May. The composer in person conducted the performance of his work, and, on entering the orchestra, was received with acclamations, in which the performers joined. The whole piece was loudly applauded, and the scherzo and trio were called for a second time. A letter, addressed immediately afterwards to the Secretary, gracefully acknowledging the Society's kindness, is characteristic of his modest nature :—" I deeply feel," he said, " the honour of which the Philharmonic Society has deemed me worthy, in performing a symphony of my composition at the last concert, an honour which I can never forget. I know that my success, obtained through the brilliant execution of the orchestra, is due much less to my talent than to the indulgence shown to my youth; but, encouraged by a reception so flattering, I shall labour to justify the hopes entertained of me, to which I undoubtedly owe the kind feeling shown to me."* At the same

---

* " J'ai senti vivement l'honneur dont la Société Philharmonique m'a jugé digne en voulant bien faire exécuter à son dernier concert une simphonie de ma composition. J'en conserverai toujours le souvenir. Je sais que ce succès, obtenu surtout grâce à la brillante exécution de l'orchestre, je le dois bien moins à mon talent, qu' à l'indulgence que m'a value ma jeunesse ; mais encouragé par un témoignage si flatteur, je travaillerai à justifier les espérances qu'on a bien voulu former, et auxquelles je dois sans doute la bienveillance que l'on m'a montrée." Though this letter was written in French, Mendelssohn even then was well acquainted with our language, and in a short time wrote and spoke it with the purity and fluency of a native.

time he sent the manuscript of the symphony, requesting permission to dedicate it to the Society as a mark of his gratitude; and accordingly the symphony was published with a dedication to the Philharmonic Society of London. At the general meeting of November 29, 1829, he was unanimously elected an Honorary Member of this Society.

The last concert of this season was remarkable for the first performance of Spohr's fine symphony in E flat, and likewise for the brilliancy of the vocal part of the entertainment, the singers being the great rivals Sontag and Malibran, both of them at that time in the full blaze of their fame. Sontag sang Mercadante's aria, "Del mio pianto," Malibran the finale to the Cenerentola; and they sang together the great duet, " Ebben a te, ferisci," from *Semiramide*. These ladies having offered their services on this occasion, the thanks of the Society were accompanied by an elegant piece of plate presented to each.

On the 6th of February, 1830, the Argyle

Rooms were destroyed by fire. The fire was discovered about ten o'clock at night, and in a few hours the whole building was reduced to ashes. A great quantity of valuable property was consumed, but happily the Library of the Philharmonic Society was saved. Mr. D'Almaine, Mr. Frederick Beale, Mr. R. Cocks, Mr. Ford and Mr. Sherrington were immediately on the spot, and, by their exertions, the contents of the Library were conveyed to the warehouse of Mr. Cocks, who kindly took charge of them. The Directors immediately made a proposal to M. Laporte, the lessee of the Italian Opera-house, to engage the concert-room belonging to that theatre for the season about to begin, and a bargain to that effect was accordingly concluded. There the concerts continued to be given till the year 1833, when they were removed to their present locality, the Hanover Square Rooms.

At the first concert of this season (1830), Mendelssohn's overture to the *Midsummer Night's Dream* was performed for the first time, the parts having been copied from the manuscript score which had been presented to Sir George Smart by the composer. Its exquisite lightness and beauty, truly Shakesperian fancy, and novelty of effect, excited a strong sensation, and the audience expressed their delight by the most vehement applause. At the sixth concert Mendelssohn's symphony in C minor, produced the previous season, was repeated. At the third concert Hummel's concerto in E, called *Les Adieux à Paris* was performed with great effect by Mr. Neate; and, at the eighth concert, the same composer's septet in D minor was most brilliantly executed, the principal performer being Mrs. Anderson, with Messrs. Nicholson, Willman, Platt, Moralt, Lindley, and Dragonetti. At this concert M. de Beriot played one of his own concertos, which, in addition to its more legitimate beauties, was remarkable for his marvellous execution of some of the brilliant *tours de force* introduced by Paganini. At this concert, moreover, Signor Lablache (who had recently arrived in London, and appeared with *éclat* at the Opera in the character of *Figaro*, a character which he soon afterwards abandoned for that of Doctor Bartholo), sang the Barber's aria, "Largo al Factotum," with great success.

The most remarkable occurrence of the season, 1831, was the performance at the third concert of a selection from Spohr's oratorio, *The Last Judgment*, a work then new to this country, it having been performed for the first time in this country, with an English version of the words by Mr. Edward Taylor, at the Norwich Festival of the preceding season. This selection formed the first part of the concert. The principal singers were Mr. and Mrs. W. Knyvett, Mr. Vaughan, and Mr. Taylor. The chorus was select, but deficient in strength. This was a solitary instance of an oratorio performance at a Philharmonic concert, for which it was not well suited. But the Sacred Harmonic Society did not then exist, and performances of this kind were rare in London, so that it was natural for the

Directors to desire to bring before the subscribers a great work as yet almost unknown in England.

During this season Hummel paid his first visit to this country. He appeared before the Philharmonic audience on the 23rd of May, and performed his *Fantaisie Caractéristique sur un air Indien d'Obéron*, and was received in the manner due to his genius and reputation. On the 6th of June, Onslow's sextuor for the piano, flute, clarinet, horn, bassoon, and double bass, was played by Mrs. Anderson, Mr. Nicholson, Mr. Willman, Mr. Platt, Mr. Mackintosh, and Signor Dragonetti. The work, thus executed, was found to be very effective.

The celebrated John Field of St. Petersburg visited London during the season of 1832; and, at the first Philharmonic concert of that season, performed one of his own concertos. He was the favourite pupil of Clementi. Having left England at an early age and settled in the Russian capital, he had been for thirty years absent from his native country.

He was received on this occasion with great distinction, and was found equal to his high reputation. His concerto in E flat was found to be clear, symmetrical, melodious, and in a style somewhat older than that of the day; while as a pianist he reminded the audience of his illustrious master. At the second concert, a fantasia concertante, composed for the Society by the Chevalier Neukomm, for flute, oboë, clarinet, bassoon, horn, trumpet, and double bass, was performed with great success. At the fourth concert Mr. Moscheles acted for the first time as conductor, and his own symphony in C, No. 1, was performed. It was well received, especially the andante and the minuet and trio, which were much applauded. But the symphony is not a species of composition which Moscheles has cultivated; this, as far as I am aware, being the only work of its class which he has publicly produced.

At the sixth concert, Mendelssohn's overture, *The Isles of Fingal*, was performed for the first time. The idea of this striking piece of descriptive music was suggested to the composer, during his visit to Scotland, by the wild desolate scenery and stormy seas of the islands on the north-western coast. It at once created a great sensation—a sensation, we need scarcely add, that has not been diminished by numberless repetitions. At a general meeting of the Society on the 7th of June, 1832, Sir George Smart read a letter from Mendelssohn, requesting the Society's acceptance of the score of this overture; and it was resolved to present him with a piece of plate in token of the Society's thanks, which was forthwith done.

At the seventh concert, Mendelssohn made his first appearance at these concerts as a performer. He played his pianoforte concerto in G minor so much to the delight of the audience, that, by general desire, it was repeated at the eighth concert, and received with undiminished enthusiasm. At this eighth concert a symphony by Onslow, dedicated to the Philharmonic Society, was performed for the first time in this country; and the concert terminated with the overture to the *Midsummer Night's Dream*.

At the general meeting on the 5th of November, 1832, the following resolution was unanimously passed :—

"That Mr. Mendelssohn Bartholdy be requested to compose a symphony, an overture, and a vocal piece for the Society, for which he be offered the sum of one hundred guineas.

"That the copyright of the above compositions shall revert to the author after the expiration of two years; the Society reserving to itself the power of performing them at all times: it being understood that Mr. Mendelssohn have the privilege of publishing any arrangement of them as soon as he may think fit after their first performance at the Philharmonic Concerts."

This resolution having been transmitted to Mendelssohn at Berlin, he acknowledged its receipt by the following letter addressed to Mr. Watts, the Society's Secretary, dated November 28, 1832 :—

"DEAR SIR,

"I am very much obliged to you for transmitting to me the resolution passed on 5th November, at the Meeting of the Philharmonic Society. I beg you will be so kind as to express my sincerest acknowledgments and my warmest thanks for the gratifying manner in which the Society has been pleased to remember me. I feel highly honoured by the offer the Society has made, and I shall compose, according to the request, a symphony, an overture, and a vocal piece, under the conditions mentioned in the resolution. When they are finished, I hope to be able to bring them over myself, and to express in person my thanks to the Society. I beg you will let me know whether my compositions are expected to be ready for the next Season, or whether the arrangements for it are made already without them. At all events I shall lose no time, and I need not say how happy I shall be in thinking that I write for the Philharmonic Society."

On Mendelssohn's arrival in London in the spring of 1833, he wrote to the Society's Secretary on the 27th of April:—" I beg you will inform the Directors of the Philharmonic Society that the scores of my new symphony and overture are at their disposal, and that I shall be able to offer them a vocal composition in a short time hence, which will complete the three works they have done me the honour to desire me to write for the Society. But as I have finished two new overtures since last year, I beg to leave the choice to the Directors as to which they would prefer for their concerts;

and in case they should think both of them convenient for performance, I beg to offer them this fourth composition as a sign of my gratitude for the pleasure and honour they have again conferred upon me."

This communication having been duly acknowledged, with thanks for the liberal offer respecting the overtures, the Directors expressed their wish that the new symphony should be performed at the sixth concert, on the 13th of May; they begged him at the same time to perform a solo piece, and likewise to conduct the concert. At that concert, accordingly, the symphony in A major (which has been generally distinguished by the title of *The Italian Symphony*) was performed for the first time under his own direction; and he likewise performed Mozart's pianoforte concerto in D minor. His new overture (in C) was produced at the last concert of the season.

At the beginning of this season, 1833, the concerts were transferred to the Hanover Square Rooms, where they have taken place ever since. The following new pieces (besides those of Mendelssohn) were produced during the season :—a MS. quintetto for the pianoforte and stringed instruments, composed for these concerts by Mr. John Cramer ; a grand pianoforte septetto composed for the Society by Mr. Moscheles ; a fantasia drammatica by the Chevalier Neukomm ; and a new symphony in A minor by Mr. Potter. This last work was remarkably effective in performance, and the critics agreed in describing it as one of the most masterly productions of the composer.

At the general meeting of the Society on the 5th of November, 1832, when Mr. Mendelssohn was requested to compose certain works for the Society, Mr. Bishop was requested to compose a concerted vocal piece, Mr. Cramer a concerted piece for the pianoforte, and Mr. Potter and Mr. J. H. Griesbach a symphony each. And at another meeting on the 12th of the same month, similar requests of instrumental and vocal compositions were made to the Chevalier Neukomm, Mr. Moscheles, and Mr. Griffin ; the conditions being the same as those offered to Mr. Mendelssohn. In consequence of these requests, the compositions above mentioned, viz., Mr. Cramer's quintetto, Mr. Moscheles's septetto, the Chevalier Neukomm's fantasia, and Mr. Potter's symphony, were produced and performed during the season 1833. A sacred cantata by Mr. Bishop, entitled "The Seventh Day," was performed at the first concert of the season 1834. It is an elaborate and masterly work in the oratorio style, and was carefully performed, the solo parts being sung by Mrs. Bishop, Miss Clara Novello, Mr. Horncastle, and Mr. E. Taylor. It was well received, but made no lasting impression; belonging to a class of music widely different from that in which Bishop has achieved a fame akin to that of Purcell and Arne. At the second concert, an Italian dramatic cantata, entitled "Rosalba," by Mr. Novello, in which the principal part was sung by Miss Clara Novello, was performed with considerable success. At the third concert, Moscheles's *Concerto Fantasique* was performed for the first time by the composer. The programme of this concert also included a new motet, *Exaltabo*, by Mr. Horsley, Mendelssohn's overture to *Melusine*, (performed for the first time,) and Mr. J. H. Griesbach's MS. overture to *Belshazzar's Feast.* At the fifth concert Ries's *Overture et Marche Triumphale* was introduced, and Beethoven's violin concerto was performed by Mr. Mori. At the seventh concert, the second part commenced with Mendelssohn's symphony in A, first produced the previous season; and at the eighth concert Mrs. Anderson performed Beethoven's concerto in E flat, and a solo was played by Madame Filipowicz, a female violinist.

The production of Spohr's great descriptive symphony, *Die Weihe der Töne*, inaugurated the season of 1835. It formed the commencement of the first concert, and was conducted by Mr. George Smart. Its subject was suggested by Pfeiffer's "Ode to Music;" the composer having attempted to illustrate, by means of musical sounds, the various descriptions and images contained in that poem. His design is shown by the programme of the symphony, which is as follows: "*First Movement:* the deep silence of nature before the creation of sound—the awakening of life after it—the voice of nature—the uproar of the elements. *Second Movement:* Cradle Song—The Dance—The Serenade. *Third Movement:* Martial music—March to battle—Return of the conquerors. *Fourth Movement:* Funeral dirge—Consolation in grief." It is easy to perceive that this design is highly suggestive of musical expression and effect; and the symphony, which, as a whole, is of colossal proportions, is full of powerful and beautiful passages. It met, especially at first, with much criticism; and the apparent — for it is only apparent — absurdity of representing, by means of sound, the deep silence of nature before sound existed, was not spared. But the work has stood the test of time, and is generally regarded as one of the author's greatest achievements.

The name of our admirable violinist, Henry Blagrove, first appears in the programme of this concert. He played a concerto of Molique with great success. At a subsequent concert of this season (the sixth), another highly distinguished English musician made his first appearance as a composer and pianist, namely, William Sterndale Bennett, who played his own concerto in E flat, produced the year before at the Royal Academy of Music; the author being about the age of seventeen, and then a student.

The following were the principal novelties of the season 1836 : First concert — Mendelssohn's overture, *Meerestille* (The calm sea and prosperous voyage) ; second concert — Beethoven's concerto in G, played by Mrs. Anderson ; third concert — Weber's *Concert-stück*, played by Madame Dulcken ; fourth concert— Mozart's concerto in C minor, Mr. Potter ; fifth concert—Mr. Sterndale Bennett's concerto in C minor, played by himself; sixth concert—fantasia performed by Thalberg ; eighth concert — another performance by him, and a cantata by

Bishop, "The departure from Paradise," sung by Madame Malibran.

This season the Society was for the first time deprived of the services of the singers of the Italian Opera. The programme of the fifth concert (April 25, 1836) contains the following announcement : "The Directors, anxious to afford the subscribers all the advantages in their power, applied for Mr. Laporte's permission to engage the principal vocal performers of the King's Theatre, which has been refused." Mr. Laporte's example has been generally followed by his successors in the management of that theatre, and also by the managers of the Royal Italian Opera. Before that time, all the great stars of the Italian stage regularly appeared at the Philharmonic concerts.

The principal occurrence of the year 1837 was the reproduction of Beethoven's ninth, or Choral Symphony. It was performed at the fourth concert, on the 17th of April. It was now much better understood than before, both by the orchestra and the public. The excessively difficult choral and concerted vocal music was sung with effect, the solo performers being Mrs. Bishop, Miss Hawes, Mr. Horncastle, and Mr. Phillips. Its beauties were now fully recognised, and it was listened to with the warmest demonstrations of pleasure.

Among other objects of interest presented by the concerts of this season, were Moscheles's concerto in C minor, performed by himself; Weber's concerto for the clarinet, played by Mr. Willman; Mendelssohn's pianoforte concerto, performed by Madame Dulcken; an "Introduction and Fugue" for full orchestra by Mozart, never performed in this country: and Sterndale Bennett's overture, *The Naiades*.

Of the season 1838, the most remarkable pieces were, Mendelssohn's pianoforte concerto composed for the Birmingham Festival, performed by Mrs. Anderson; Moscheles's *Concerto Pathétique* played by himself; Beethoven's *Choral Symphony*; a pianoforte fantasia, performed by Dohler, a pianist then in vogue, of the Thalberg school; a repetition of Spohr's symphony, *Die Weihe der Töne;* and Sterndale Bennett's concerto in F minor,* performed by the composer at the eighth concert.

In the season 1839, Mendelssohn's pianoforte concerto above mentioned was performed by Madame Dulcken; Sterndale Bennett produced his overtures *Parisina* and *The Wood Nymphs,* and his concerto in F minor, op. 19; Moscheles performed his *Pastoral Concerto;* Herr David, the eminent violinist of Leipzig, performed a concerto of his own with great success; Mr. H. Blagrove played Spohr's *Dramatic Concerto,* and was much applauded; Madame Dorus Gras appeared at two concerts, and created a great sensation by her brilliant execution, especially in Auber's music; Mario made his first appearance in London—he sang at two concerts, a French romance of Niedermayer and an air from Meyerbeer's *Crociato,* and pleased, though without showing the powers he afterwards displayed on the stage.

In 1840 two symphonies of Spohr were

---

* Unpublished.

performed for the first time. The one was his No. 5, performed at the first concert without producing much effect. The other was his *Historical Symphony* then in manuscript; a work, the design of which was to illustrate the progress of orchestral music by specimens of the style of the greatest composers from the year 1720 to the present time. It was coldly received, and met with a similar reception when repeated in 1849. Notwithstanding the masterly skill and learning displayed in this composition, the objections to its design, made by the critics at the time, are obviously just. It is useless to give imitations of Bach, Handel, Haydn, Mozart, and Beethoven, when their actual works are well known; and the introduction of such various styles into one work must render it *patchy* and incoherent.

At the second concert of this season, Mrs. Anderson again performed Mendelssohn's concerto written for the Birmingham Festival. At the third concert M. Molique made his first public appearance in England; he performed a concerto of his own composition, and was most warmly applauded. His reception was so favourable that he was requested to perform another of his concertos at the subsequent concert, and likewise a fantasia at the fifth.

Liszt appeared several times this season. He played Weber's *Concert-stück,* Beethoven's *Kreutzer Sonata* (with M. Ole Bull), and a solo containing his celebrated *Marche Hongroise.* His great powers of execution were much applauded, especially in his own music, but his reading of the text of Weber and Beethoven was not approved by the more critical portion of the audience. A fantasia by M. Ole Bull, consisting of variations on a Norwegian air, was interesting from the plaintive expression and national character of the theme, but the variations were little more than a string of extravagant feats of execution *à la* Paganini.

At the second concert of the year 1841 Mendelssohn's *Lobgesang,* or Hymn of Praise, formed the second act of the performance. This work had been brought out at the Birmingham Festival of the preceding year, for which it was expressly written. Its reproduction by the Philharmonic Society had not the effect which might have been expected from the impression it had made at Birmingham. But it was not then discovered by experience, as it has been since, that choral performances of sacred music are unsuitable to the Philharmonic concerts, the limited dimensions of the room rendering it impossible to get up such performances on a scale of sufficient magnitude. The *Lobgesang* is now well known to the public, having been repeatedly heard, in all its grandeur, at Exeter Hall, the only locality fitted for such music which London at present possesses.

At this concert the English public had the first specimen of the music of Berlioz. His overture to his opera, *Benvenuto Cellini*, was performed, and received with little favour; and the opera itself, it may be remembered, was received with still less, several years afterwards, at the Royal Italian Opera, where it failed to obtain a second hearing. It may be added, however, that some of his orchestral works have since met with better success in London; the real beauties, mingled with his peculiarities and extravagancies, having become more apparent.

The third concert had this peculiarity, that the vocal music consisted wholly of concerted pieces. There were Dr. Crotch's fine sestetto from *Palestine*, "Lo, cherub bands;" Meyerbeer's quintetto, "O cielo clemente," from the *Crociato*; the terzetto, "Giovinetto Cavalier," from the same opera; and Spohr's quintetto, "Zemira, children, all draw near," from *Azor and Zemira*. The singers were Miss Birch, Miss Woodyatt, Miss Hawes, Mr. Hobbs, Mr. J. L. Hatton, and Mr. Machin. The rich stores of concerted music, in all the vocal schools of Europe, might be turned to greater account than the Philharmonic directors have generally been in the habit of doing. Many dramatic concerted pieces, indeed, lose their effect when brought from the stage to the concert-room;

but this objection applies with equal force to those pieces for a single voice—those operatic scenas which are heard at almost every concert. The thing to consider, in selecting a vocal piece, is, not whether it is for one voice or for many, but whether it can be sung at a concert without detriment to its design and meaning—a question, it would seem, which concert-makers very seldom ask.

Vieuxtemps appeared at three of the concerts of this season. He performed two concertos composed by himself, and played the leading part in one of Beethoven's quintets for stringed instruments. His own compositions were not calculated to do justice to his powers; their great length created impatience, and his execution had not yet acquired the fine finish of his after days; but in Beethoven's quintet he gained every suffrage by his purity of style and respect for the composer's text; a style very different from that of M. Liszt in his performance at the same concert of the pianoforte part of Hummel's septetto, this great but eccentric performer having embellished Hummel's passages in such a way that their author himself could scarcely have known them.

The season of 1842 was chiefly remarkable for the production of two new works by the great symphonists of the age, Spohr and Mendelssohn. Spohr's symphony, "Descriptive of the conflict of Virtue and Vice in Man," was performed at the sixth, and Mendelssohn's symphony in A minor at the seventh concert.* In Spohr's symphony, the author seems to have carried what may be called the "metaphysical style" to a greater length than in any of his other works. It is in three parts or movements. In the first, entitled "Infancy," the freedom of that happy age from bad and stormy passions is endeavoured to be painted; the second, called the "Age of Sorrows," paints the evil passions and influences of manhood; and the last, the "Final Triumph of Virtue," describes the calm of virtue and devotion after the turmoils of "life's fitful fever" have passed away.

* See Appendix.

It is evident, from the mere mention of the subject of this symphony, that Spohr, with all his knowledge of the philosophy of his art, mistook, in this instance, its powers and objects, endeavouring to employ it in the expression of abstract ideas and moral sentiments, to which musical sounds have no greater analogy than to the demonstration of a proposition of Euclid. In the technical construction, too, of this symphony, there is a peculiarity which did not prove effective. It is of the nature of a concertante, there being a body of eleven solo performers detached from the general orchestra. This, in truth, was a revival of the antique form of the orchestral concerto, the precursor of the symphony, in which the *concerto grosso* or the passages for the full band, alternated with the *concertino*, passages excuted by a small select body of solo instruments. In Spohr's symphony, though the eleven performers were placed in front of the orchestra, they did not stand out from the background of the picture in the clear and prominent relief contemplated by the composer, and indeed no effect was produced which could not have been accomplished by means of an ordinary orchestra. A work from such a pen must have many beauties, but, as a whole, it must be deemed the unsuccessful experiment of a great master.

Mendelssohn's symphony in A minor is also an essay of the descriptive powers of music; but these powers are employed legitimately, and within the domain of the art. It was suggested by the impressions made upon the composer by the national music of Scotland during his visit to that country in 1829. At Edinburgh he was present at the annual "Competition of Pipers," where the most renowned performers on the great Highland Bagpipe—feudal retainers of the chiefs of clans, pipers of Scottish regiments, &c.—contend for prizes, in the presence of a great assemblage of the rank and fashion of the northern capital. He was greatly interested by the war-tunes of the different clans, and the other specimens of the music of the country which he heard on that occasion, and during his tour through various parts of Scotland ; and in this symphony, though composed long afterwards, he embodied some of his reminiscences of a period to which he always looked back with pleasure.* The delightful manner in which he has reproduced some of the most characteristic features of the national music—solemn, pathetic, gay, and warlike—is familiar to every amateur.

On this memorable evening Mendelssohn appeared for the first time before the public in the capacity of conductor of the orchestra ; directing not only the performance of his own symphony, but the entire concert. The room was crowded to overflowing with the *élite* of our artistic society, and he was received with an enthusiasm impossible to describe.

---

* It will be deemed, I hope, a pardonable piece of egotism when I mention that I had the happiness to be his companion at the "Competition of Pipers," and on some other occasions when he heard Scottish music, and that it was with pride and pleasure that I observed the interest he took in the melodies of my country.

At the subsequent concert (the eighth) Mendelssohn played his concerto in D minor, and conducted the performance of his overture, *The Isles of Fingal.*

In the season 1843, at the second concert, a concerto of Chopin was played by Madame Dulcken; this being the first public performance in this country of any of the music of this composer, whose beautiful and original mazurkas and other *morceaux de salon* are now well known to the public. At the third concert two great works of Beethoven were performed, similar in their peculiar combination of instrumental and choral effects:—his fantasia for the pianoforte, orchestra, and chorus; and his ninth, or *Choral Symphony* In the fantasia the pianoforte part was played by Mrs. Anderson; in both pieces the solo vocal parts were sung by Madame Caradori Allan, Miss Hawes, Mr. Hobbs, and Mr. Phillips; and the chorus was a hundred strong. At the fourth concert, M. Dreyschock made his first appearance in this country, performing a fantasia of his own, and surprising the audience by his brilliant execution and the novel effects he drew from the instrument. The fifth concert was again of a choral character: Beethoven's fantasia, performed at the third concert, was repeated in the same manner as before; and the second act of the concert consisted of Mendelssohn's *Lobgesang*, which had been first performed during the season of 1841. At the sixth concert, Sterndale Bennett's *Concert-stück* in A minor was performed, for the first time, by the composer; and Camillo Sivori made his first appearance in England, playing a concerto of his own. At the seventh concert Sivori appeared again, performing another of his own concertos; and Mendelssohn's concerto in G minor was played by Madame Belleville Oury. Of the eighth concert the chief feature was the personal presence of Spohr, who performed one of his own concertos, and conducted the performance of his great symphony *Die Weihe der Töne*, his overture to the *Alchymist*, and a duet from his *Jessonda*, sung by Miss Birch and

Miss Masson. It is hardly necessary to add that he was welcomed by a crowded audience with every mark of cordiality and respect.

There was an extra concert on the 10th of July given by command of the Queen, at which Her Majesty and the Prince Consort were accompanied by the King of the Netherlands. The whole of this concert was conducted by Dr. Spohr: its programme included Mendelssohn's overture, *The Isles of Fingal;* the chorus, " Oh, great is the depth," from *St. Paul;* the scherzo and second part of Beethoven's *Choral Symphony,* Mozart's symphony in D, an air from *Jessonda* (sung by Staudigl), one of Spohr's concertos, and his overture to *Macbeth.*

At the first concert of the year 1844, Sir George Smart acted for the last time in the capacity of conductor. Though there was no formal announcement of this, yet it had become known to the public ; and, on Sir George's leaving the orchestra at the end of the concert, he was loudly applauded both by the audience and the orchestra,—a just tribute of esteem and respect for his high character, his great talents, and his long and important services to the cause of Music in this country.

The Directors having determined to offer Dr. Mendelssohn an engagement as conductor of six concerts of this season, the proposal was communicated to him by the Secretary. His letter of acceptance, dated Berlin, the 4th of March, is as follows :—

"SIR,

"I beg to acknowledge the receipt of your letter dated February 27th, and express my sincere and best thanks to the Philharmonic Society for the honourable and handsome offer contained therein. I am happy to say that I have since yesterday the certainty of being able to accept it, and that I intend to set out on my journey immediately after Easter, when my engagements allow me to leave this place. I am not quite sure whether I shall reach England in time for the third concert (29th April), although I hope and intend to do so: but at any rate I shall be there for the last five concerts; and it is with a feeling of true gratitude, and with the anticipation of a great musical treat, that I say this, and beg you will thank the Society in my name, until I shall be able to do so in person. There are many questions and details about which I write to Mr. Bennett, and beg to enclose this letter to him." *

---

* See Appendix.

He arrived in time for the fourth concert, and acted as conductor for the remainder of the season. Nothing could be more harmonious than his intercourse with the Directors. He attended their meetings, gave them his advice and assistance in their arrangements, and showed the warmest interest in the success of the concerts and the welfare of the Society. He enjoyed in the highest degree the confidence and good will of the orchestra, who were proud of his approbation and zealous in their endeavours to satisfy and please him in everything.

The second concert of this season was the occasion on which Ernst made his first appearance in England. He played Spohr's dramatic concerto and his own fantasia on themes from the *Pirata*; making an impression fully maintained by many subsequent visits to this country, till his failing health most unhappily interrupted his artistic career. Let us hope that the interruption is only temporary, and that we may yet enjoy the pleasure of hearing from his instrument those tones which, for romantic beauty and pathetic expression, never have been excelled. At the fourth concert Beethoven's overture to *Leonora* was performed for the first time in this country. This overture was rejected by the composer, on the revival of his opera under the title of *Fidelio*, to make way for the overture in E, which has ever since been always attached to the opera. But, though not so well fitted for the theatre, the overture to *Leonora* is by far the superior work; and in the concert-room its large proportions and grand style almost gave it the importance of a symphony. At the fifth concert, Joseph Joachim, then a boy of thirteen, made his first appearance, and performed Beethoven's concerto in a manner which astonished and delighted the audience, and justified the splendid reputation which, even at that early age, he had achieved throughout Europe. This concert was also rendered remarkable by the performance of the portions of Mendelssohn's music in *The*

Midsummer Night's Dream which had not been heard before in England; those portions (in addition to the overture) being the instrumental scherzo, the two-part song with chorus, "Ye spotted snakes," the notturno, wedding march, and final chorus. This delicious music was admirably performed, the two-part song being sung by Miss Rainforth and Miss A. Williams, and rapturously received, the composer, who was acting as conductor, being greeted with acclamations. This reception led to its repetition at the subsequent concert. It has been repeated many times since, and always with the same effect on the audience. At the seventh concert Mendelssohn played Beethoven's concerto in G; and our admirable violoncellist, Piatti, made his first appearance, performing a concerto of Kummer. If we may judge from the recorded language of some eminent critics, his great powers were not immediately recognised by the self-constituted directors of public taste, but even they soon fell into the general current of opinion as to the merits of this great artist. The last concert was marked by the production of *The First Walpurgis Night.* Performed under the author's own direction, with Miss A. Williams, Miss Dolby, Mr. Allen, and M. Staudigl in the solo vocal parts, and with the aid of a powerful and well-disciplined chorus, this great and very original work was given with the utmost possible effect. It is now too well known to the public to require a word of remark. Another feature of this concert was the performance of a selection from Beethoven's *Ruins of Athens,* a work then unknown in this country, but since rendered familiar to the public by many repetitions.

Sir Henry Bishop was engaged as conductor of the concerts for the season of 1845; but, after having conducted three concerts, he found it necessary, in consequence of the state of his health, to resign the office; and Mr. Moscheles was engaged to conduct the remaining concerts of the season.

This season presents few remarkable features;

and indeed I may observe that, from this period a marked diminution is apparent in the production of new compositions. All the noted works of the great orchestral composers, dead and living, up to this time, had been brought forward; and the supply of new works of this description had begun to fail. There was no lack, indeed, of symphonies, concertos, overtures, and other instrumental pieces, constantly produced throughout Europe; but there was no longer a Haydn, a Mozart, a Beethoven, a Weber, a Spohr, or a Mendelssohn to produce them; and the line of these illustrious men has not been continued by successors of kindred genius. The Philharmonic Society has often been blamed for not seeking laboriously everything that can be found throughout the world of music, and giving to the public the fruits of their researches, however inferior these may be. At all events, it has been said, they are new; and novelty and variety are better than a narrow round of things, which, however excellent, have been rendered stale by constant repetition. The Society, fortunately, I apprehend, has judged differently. The existing works of the great masters form a repertory so extensive as to be indeed inexhaustible; and when a successor to Mendelssohn shall appear, it will be time to add new masterpieces to those which we possess already.

During the season of 1845 the only new orchestral work of merit and importance was Macfarren's symphony in C sharp minor; and the only new performers whose appearance created interest were the two charming sisters, Teresa and Maria Milanollo, who were at that time enchanting all Europe with their violin-playing, which completely dispelled the prejudice that the violin is either unsuited to female powers or unbecoming in female hands. Their "fiddling" was as graceful and feminine as it was wonderful and delightful.

In 1846, Signor Costa was engaged as conductor. From this time the title of "Leader" disappeared from the programmes, and the term "Principal" was appended to the names of the performers which stood highest in the lists of first and second violins, violoncellos, tenors, and double-basses. Signor Costa had long held the situation of musical director at Her Majesty's Theatre, and his actual experience as a *chef d'orchestre* was limited to the music of the Italian stage. But his talents and energy in this new sphere of duty justified the choice of the Directors ; for he discharged his functions in a manner as satisfactory to the Society and the public as to the members of the orchestra. He held his office for eight years—till the end of the season 1854.

The most remarkable occurrence of the season 1846, was the production of Beethoven's *Missa Solennis* in D, the most colossal work of its class, which, like the equally colossal ninth symphony, was one of the author's great efforts in the latest period of his life. Its composition was undertaken with the view of its being performed on the occasion of a certain public solemnity ; but the solemnity took place before the mass was complete. At the great concert got up for Beethoven's benefit in 1824, by the Austrian aristocracy, by way of compensation for the neglect with which they had always treated him, a portion of this mass was performed, I believe, for the first time, along with the *Choral Symphony*. It was given entire, and on a grand scale, on the festival in honour of Beethoven, at Bonn, in 1845; but its repetitions have been few and far between, even in Germany. Its performance by the Philharmonic Society was got up with very great care. The four solo vocal parts were doubled; the soprani being Miss S. Novello and Miss A. Williams; the contralti, Miss M. Williams and Miss Steele; the tenors, Mr. Lockey and Mr. R. Costa; the basses, Signor F. Lablache and Mr. A. Novello. The chorus was a hundred strong, and composed of the best attainable voices; correctness was gained by numerous extra rehearsals; and the result was a performance which satisfied the most severe critics, and did great honour to the Society. Its effect on the audience generally, however, was not commensurate with the pains and labour bestowed upon it; for, independently of the depth and novelty of its construction and style, it is one of those works which cannot be heard to advantage unless in a cathedral or other locality where its vast proportions can be fully developed.*

During this season the following orchestral pieces were performed for the first time :— Spohr's symphony in D, Op. 49, composed for and dedicated to this Society; Mr. Lucas's overture to *The Regicide*;† and Mendelssohn's violin concerto, performed by Signor Sivori. Moreover, Weber's *Concert-stück* was performed by the celebrated pianist, Madame

---

* At the two recent performances of this mass by the Sacred Harmonic Society, at Exeter Hall, it was clothed in all its grandeur and sublimity.

† This opera stands in the singular position of being published without having been performed. The drama is an English version of Metastasio's *Artaserse;* a version greatly superior to that made by Dr. Arne for his *Artaxerxes*. Both these circumstances were adverse to the popularity of the music, though it has much merit, containing several fine airs and concerted scenes of great dramatic effect.

Pleyel; and Madame Dulcken played a pianoforte concerto (MS.), of Parish Alvars.

In 1847, Mendelssohn came to England for the last time. He conducted the fourth concert of the season, which included his symphony in A minor, and his music in the *Midsummer Night's Dream.* He performed, moreover, Beethoven's concerto in G. Soon afterwards he took a last farewell of his English friends. His health, at the time of his departure, was evidently giving way; and he died, after a long and lingering illness, on the 4th day of the following month of November.

The most remarkable concert of the year 1848 was the third, on the 10th of April; a day memorable for the alarming " demonstration of physical force " made by the Chartists, under Mr. Feargus O'Connor. Notwithstanding the agitation which had prevailed throughout London, the concert was better attended than might have been expected, and the audience did not fail to express the loyal feelings of British subjects. At the end of the first part, "God Save the Queen" was performed by the orchestra and chorus, and received with a degree of enthusiasm rarely witnessed. At the words, "Confound their politics!" the whole company burst into acclamations of triumph, accompanied with the waving of hats and handkerchiefs, which drowned the sounds of the voices and instruments. This concert was also remarkable in a musical point of view. It included Mendelssohn's vocal quartet and chorus from Schiller's poem "To the Sons of Art." It is a beautiful and original work, consisting of several stanzas, each sung by four unaccompanied voices, and repeated in chorus accompanied by all the brass instruments, with a novel and imposing effect. It is somewhat surprising that this work has never been repeated. This concert also included Meyerbeer's overture to *Struensee*, performed for the first time in this country, and Beethoven's "Chorus of Dervishes," from *The Ruins of Athens*. The other most remarkable performances of this season were, Mr. J. H.

Griesbach's overture to *Titania*—a masterly work; Beethoven's concerto in E flat, played by Mrs. Anderson; Beethoven's in C minor, performed by Madame Dulcken; a pianoforte concerto, composed and performed by M. Prudent; Mendelssohn's concerto in G minor, performed by Miss Kate Loder, then commencing her short but brilliant career; and last, but not least, Spohr's new MS. symphony, No. 8, composed for the Philharmonic Society.

The most interesting occurrence of the season 1849, was the production of "The Lyrics of Racine's *Athalie*," composed by Mendelssohn. Racine's celebrated tragedy, it will be remembered, partly belongs to the lyrical stage. The characters of the drama act and speak in the usual manner; but there are certain situations in which assemblages of the people, and of the priests and attendants of the temple, are introduced. These scenes are written in lyrical measures, like the choruses of the ancient Greek tragedy, and were performed with choral and concerted music, which is lost and forgotten.

Placed at the end of the acts, these scenes resemble a good deal the finales to the acts of a modern grand opera. The tragedy was written with the view of being performed, or rather recited, by the young ladies of Madame de Maintenon's celebrated seminary of Saint Cyr; but it could not have received all its dramatic and musical adjuncts till it came to be represented in a public theatre. In the year 1846, a German version of the tragedy was produced with great splendour at Berlin, Mendelssohn having composed music for the lyrical portions, to be introduced according to Racine's own original design. The sensation created by this remarkable occurrence attracted the attention of our Queen and the Prince Consort; and accordingly a performance of the lyrical scenes took place at Windsor on New Year's Day, 1847; the spoken part of the tragedy, much abridged, being read; so that the lyrical scenes were disjoined from each other, and, at the same time, the continuity and coherence of the piece, as a whole, was preserved.

At the first Philharmonic Concert of 1849, the lyrical portions of the tragedy were performed, but without any intermediate matter to separate those portions from each other, and to serve as connecting links between them. The inconvenience of this defect was felt; but, nevertheless, the effect of the performance was magnificent; and, Her Majesty having commanded its repetition at the following concert, the royal command was obeyed, means being taken to improve its effect very greatly. These means are explained in a note prefixed to the programme by Mr. Bartholomew, to whom, as the literary assistant of Mendelssohn, the English public is so much indebted. Mr. Bartholomew had furnished the English version of the lyrics, as performed at the first concert; and the following is his interesting explanation of the manner in which he supplied the deficiency already mentioned :—

"I had sometime ago completed an abridged English version of Racine's *Athalie,* when the idea of the following poem was suggested to me by Mr. Costa, for the purpose of being *musically* recited with its choral lyrics; but as objections were made to so close a union of other music with that of Mendelssohn, the idea was laid aside. I resumed it, on hearing that a poem had been written and declaimed by its author in Germany; and had partly completed it, when the *Zwischenreden* of Edward Devrient arrived, with the published full score of the music, in London. I then availed myself of some of its trivial points, which I considered better than those extant in mine; but in no instance, I hope, that subjects me to censure as a plagiarist. By the expedient of declaiming these verses, the whole of the beautiful music, as written by Mendelssohn for the *Athalie* of Racine, may thus be effectively performed in the concert-room; although the sanctity of the tragedy it elucidates still deprives it of many advantages it would gain by dramatic representation, for which it was composed."

At the second concert, accordingly, the intercalary verses, which narrate the incidents of the drama, were recited by the late Mr. Bartley with great clearness and beauty of elocution. Of course the effect of the lyrical scenes could not be equal to what it must have been when the entire tragedy was represented on the stage as at Berlin; but certainly the expedient now adopted was on the whole satisfactory, and will be adhered to whenever this, the last great work of Mendelssohn, is performed in this country. The solo voice parts (as at the previous concert) were sung by Miss Williams, Mrs. Noble, and Miss M. Williams. The performance was complete and finished in every respect; and the royal visitors (as well as the rest of the audience) warmly expressed the pleasure they received.*

---

   * This music has been several times performed by the Sacred Harmonic Society at Exeter Hall, the last time very recently. But it does not demand the great choral and orchestral strength which are necessary for an oratorio, and can therefore receive ample justice in a smaller locality. Undoubtedly the effect of the performances in the Hanover-

Spohr's Historical Symphony, first performed in 1840, was repeated this season, but not with increased success. The design of this composition is evidently a mistake, not redeemed by the many beauties which it contains. Beethoven's *Choral Symphony* was likewise repeated, and made a greater impression than ever. Among the most notable occurrences of the season, were the re-appearance of Ernst, after an absence of five years; Miss Kate Loder's performance of Mendelssohn's Serenade and *Allegro Giojoso*, by which that excellent young artist gathered fresh laurels; the appearance of a young female violinist, Mademoiselle Neruda, who, though only fourteen, made a great impression by her fine performance of a concerto of De Beriot; and Mozart's beautiful trio for the pianoforte, clarinet, and viola, played, to the delight of the audience,

square Rooms has not been exceeded. I venture to add a remark which is perhaps trifling. Why, in an English poem, do we preserve the French name *Athalie*, instead of the name in our own Holy Scriptures—*Athaliah?*

by Mr. Lindsay Sloper, Mr. Williams, and Mr. Hill.

At the fourth concert of this season (on the 30th of April), Mrs. Anderson performed Mendelssohn's concerto in G minor. Since that time she has not re-appeared at these concerts, much to the regret of the public, for she has shown, at her own annual concerts, that she continues to be in full possession of all her powers both mental and physical. The Philharmonic audience would hail her reappearance as warmly as ever. A few weeks later, on the 11th of June, another of our great female pianists, Madame Dulcken, appeared for the last time. The untimely death of this accomplished artist, which took place soon afterwards, was deeply and generally lamented.

In the season 1849, Mendelssohn's overture to *Ruy Blas* was performed for the first time at these concerts.* Mendelssohn's violin con-

---

* The history of this magnificent overture, in connection with the Philharmonic Society, is interesting and charac-

certo was performed by Mr. H. C. Cooper (who appeared for the first time) with great success.

teristic of the author. During the season 1844, when Mendelssohn conducted the Society's Concerts, this overture (in manuscript), was tried at a morning trial-performance, when, it would appear, it did not "go" to the composer's satisfaction. When Mr. Anderson, after the performance, expressed his admiration of the new work, he was surprised to hear Mendelssohn say, with some heat, that he was much displeased with it—so much, that he would burn it. Mr. Anderson said something deprecating such a resolution, but Mendelssohn repeated his determination that it should never be heard in public. Mr. Anderson then said : "You have often expressed your admiration of my good master, Prince Albert ; I am sure it would gratify him to hear a new composition of yours, so pray let me give him that pleasure by means of the Queen's private band." Mendelssohn consented, on condition that the overture should never be publicly performed, and gave Mr. Anderson the original orchestral parts. The overture was frequently performed at Buckingham Palace and Windsor Castle, to the admiration of Her Majesty and the Prince. Some time after the composer's lamented death, Mr. Anderson wrote to Madame Mendelssohn, informing her of all that had passed with respect to this overture, and requesting her permission to perform it at Mrs. Anderson's next annual concert. The permission was kindly given, and the overture was performed at that lady's concert in the season 1849 ; this being the first time it was ever publicly heard in England. As said above, it was afterwards performed the same season by the Philharmonic Society.

Mr. Potter's masterly symphony in D minor was performed and received with warm applause, the *andante* movement being encored. A reception not less favourable was given to Mr. Sterndale Bennett's pianoforte caprice, performed by Miss Kate Loder. M. Thalberg performed twice at the sixth concert; Mozart's concerto in D minor, and his own variations on the barcarole in the *Elisir d'Amore*. At other concerts of the season, Mr. J. H. Griesbach's overture to *The Tempest*, and Mr. Benedict's *Concert-stück* in C minor (performed by himself), were produced for the first time, and deservedly applauded. On the 20th of May the veteran Robert Lindley made his last appearance. He played, with Mr. Lucas and Mr. Howell, Corelli's favourite trio, with which he had so often delighted the public. He was most cordially greeted, and left the orchestra amid the warmest manifestations of regard from all parts of the room, in which the members of the orchestra joined.

Of the season 1851 the principal occurrences in respect to pieces and performers were :—

introduction and rondo by Mendelssohn, performed with great applause by Mr. W. H. Holmes, a member of the Society; concerto for the violin in E flat, by Mozart, played by M. Sainton, not mentioned in Mozart's own catalogue of his works, but said in the programme to have been composed in 1782; Beethoven's ninth or *Choral Symphony*, repeated; fantasia on themes from *Lucia*, composed and performed by Signor Sivori; Potter's overture to *Cymbeline*, repeated; a MS. overture by Mendelssohn, performed for the first time; and Hummel's concerto in A minor, played by Herr Pauer who appeared for the first time at these concerts, and had a highly favourable reception.

In 1852, Mendelssohn's *Walpurgis Night* was repeated; a symphony entitled *Im Freien* by Ferdinand Hiller, was produced under the composer's direction; Mr. Macfarren's overture to *Don Quixote* was performed, and instrumental solos were played by Piatti, Bottesini, Mademoiselle Clauss, Miss Kate Loder, Hallé, Sivori,

Joachim, Vieuxtemps, Pauer, and Cooper. Mademoiselle Wilhelmina Clauss, then under eighteen years of age, made a great impression by her exquisite execution of Beethoven's concerto in E flat, and Mr. Cooper performed Spohr's concerto in G with full success.

The season 1853 began with the production of a symphony by M. Gade, a young Danish composer, which had less effect than might have been expected from the continental reputation he had acquired. M. Hector Berlioz, having visited London, a selection from his works was performed under his direction. It consisted of his symphony, entitled, *Harold in Italy;* an air from his oratorio, *The Flight into Egypt,* sung by Signor Gardoni; and the orchestral piece, descriptive of a Roman carnival, which forms the introduction to the second act of his opera, *Benvenuto Cellini.* This music received a good deal of applause, but the opinions of the audience were much divided as to its merits; and the same division, with respect to Berlioz's character and rank as a composer, still, I believe, exists throughout the musical world.*

The following were the principal solo instrumental performances in the course of this season. Mrs. Jewson (the niece and pupil of Mrs. Anderson) made a most successful début in Mendelssohn's concerto in G minor. Signor Piatti performed a fine violoncello concerto composed for him by Molique. Signor Bottesini played a concerto on the contrabasso composed by himself, a marvellous display of executive power. Mr. H. Blagrove performed a concerto of Molique, one of the composer's best works, which received full justice from our excellent violinist. A MS. cantata by Sir Henry Bishop, entitled "The Departure from Paradise," was performed under the author's direction. It is for a soprano voice, and was sung by Miss Louisa Pyne. The composer and

---

* In the same season an Italian version of the abovementioned opera was produced at the Royal Italian Opera, Covent Garden, and so unfavourably received that it was withdrawn after one representation.

performer were warmly applauded. At another concert the same young singer made a great impression by the vocal and dramatic power displayed by her in the finale to Mendelssohn's unfinished opera, *Lorely.* The production, for the first time, of an unknown work of Beethoven, might have been supposed an occurrence of remarkable interest. But his cantata, *Der Preis der Tonkunst* (The Praise of Music), though performed with all possible care, was received with great coldness, and immediately forgotten, being generally deemed unworthy of the great master's name.

The season of 1854 presented a series of excellent and brilliant concerts; but there were few novelties, and these were not very successful. Two symphonies were performed for the first time, the one by M. Rosenhain, a German composer, resident in Paris, who had acquired a high reputation by his compositions for, and performances on, the pianoforte; and the other by the celebrated Robert Schumann. Both had been successful in France and Germany; but they were coldly received in the Hanover Square Rooms.

This was the last season of Mr. Costa's conductorship. Before the commencement of the following season, he unexpectedly declined to accept the renewal of his engagement which was offered him, and the Directors after much and anxious deliberation, offered the appointment to Herr Richard Wagner, the celebrated dramatic composer, by whom it was accepted. The choice did not eventually prove a happy one. During the season of 1855, Herr Wagner, though he discharged his duties with great care and assiduity, was unable to gain the confidence of the orchestra or the favour of the public. The second concert of this season included a selection from Wagner's opera, *Lohengrin*. It is impossible to judge of the character of a dramatic work by means of two or three fragments performed in a concert-room; but certainly the selected passages, chosen doubtless as being the best fitted for this mode of performance, did not seem so obscure and eccentric as the public had been led to expect, and some portions of them,—being natural, simple, and melodious,—were listened to with favour. The subsequent performance of Beethoven's *Choral Symphony* was accompanied with an "analysis" from Herr Wagner's pen, a translation of which was printed in the programme of the concert, an able and ingenious essay, showing a careful study of the work, but obscured by the ultra "æsthetic" style, peculiar to the German school of art-criticism, which only perplexes and mystifies the less subtle English mind. At another concert the overture to *Tannhaüser* was performed, under the same disadvantages which attended the other specimens of his music. The audience found its instrumentation very noisy, but were necessarily unable to form any notion of its dramatic design, and of its effect when heard in its proper place, the theatre, and as an introduction to the opera itself. One fact respecting the operas of Wagner is undoubted. Be their merits what they may, their present popularity throughout all Germany is unbounded, and affords a strong presumption in their favour. The recent failure of *Tannhaüser* when produced in a French dress at the Grand Opéra of Paris, may be cited as affording a presumption the other way. But no one can have read the accounts of this occurrence given by the Parisian journals without being convinced that the opera was driven from the stage by the efforts of a hostile cabal. The English public, in truth, is not now in a condition to form an estimate of the character of Richard Wagner.

The most remarkable occurrences of this season, beside the above, were, the last appearance at these concerts of the admirable Ernst, who has ever since been disabled by continual ill health from the exercise of his profession; the production of Mr. Lucas's symphony in B flat, an early but masterly work of the composer, which was received with well merited favour; the performance by Mr. Charles Hallé of Chopin's concerto in E minor, a work in which this composer's genius appears to less advantage than in those exquisite mazurkas and other *morceaux de salon* on which his reputation will chiefly rest ; and the repetition of Potter's excellent symphony in G minor, which experienced even a warmer reception than it had ever met with before. The season, altogether, was neither pleasant nor successful ; and, at its close, Mr. Wagner hastened to take his departure from England.

It having appeared to the annual general meeting in July, 1855, that the laws of the Society stood in need of revisal, a committee was appointed for that purpose ; and, in pursuance of their report, various alterations were enacted by the general meeting in November following. Of these alterations, that which chiefly concerned the public, was the change in the number of the concerts from eight to six ; the consequent change in the subscription for the season from four guineas to three ; and the adoption of a uniform rate of admission to non-subscribers of fifteen shillings for each concert. On this footing matters stood during the seasons

1856, 1857, 1858, and 1859. But it having been found that the above and several other alterations had not been attended with the advantages expected from them, a fresh revisal of the laws took place in the latter part of 1859, when the former number of the concerts and rate of subscription were re-adopted; the uniform price of fifteen shillings for a single concert being retained.

At the general meeting on the 19th of November, 1855, the office of conductor of the concerts was conferred upon Sterndale Bennett, who subsequently received the honour of the appointment of professor of music in the university of Cambridge. Professor Bennett entered upon his duties in the season of 1856, and has, ever since, continued to discharge them. The Philharmonic Society has reason to congratulate itself on this appointment; for not only have the concerts received much advantage from a conductor of such ability and so thoroughly possessed of the confidence of the orchestra, but the Society has derived both honour and benefit from this most important office being held by one so greatly esteemed, and of so high a reputation, not only in England but throughout Europe.*

At the first concert of the season, 1856, Madame Schumann, the celebrated pianist, made her first appearance in England; performing Beethoven's concerto in E flat, and Mendelssohn's 17 *Variations Sérieuses.* She also appeared at the second concert, when she played Mendelssohn's concerto in D minor. At the third concert, Spohr's *Dramatic Concerto* was performed by Mr. Cooper, who was entirely successful. At the fourth, there was a masterly performance of Beethoven's pianoforte concerto in G by Mr. Otto Goldschmidt. At the fifth, Miss Arabella Goddard made her

* The power of nominating the Conductor of the concerts, previously vested in the Directors, was, by the Law of 1855, transferred to the Society at a general meeting; and accordingly Professor Bennett's first nomination was made by a general meeting as above mentioned. But this power has been restored to the Directors, by whom, since 1859, Professor Bennett's appointment has been periodically renewed.

début at the Philharmonic Concerts. She performed Sterndale Bennett's concerto in C minor, and was received with enthusiastic applause. And at the sixth, which was given "by command," Schumann's cantata, *Paradise and the Peri,* was performed for the first time in this country. This concert excited great interest, enhanced by the circumstance that the principal solo part was sustained by Madame Goldschmidt (Jenny Lind), at whose suggestion (it was understood) this piece was brought forward. The concert was attended by the Queen, the late Prince Consort, several of the princes and princesses, and the foreign royal personages then on a visit to her Majesty; and the room was crowded to the doors with an assemblage including a multitude of our most noted musicians and amateurs. The words of this cantata are a German version of the well-known episode in Moore's *Lalla Rookh,* re-translated for this occasion into English by Mr. Bartholomew, who, with great skill and judgment, adhered very closely to Moore's own words. The other solo parts, besides the principal soprano, were sung by Madame Weiss, Mrs. Lockey, and Mr. Benson. The chorus was large and select, and the utmost care was bestowed on the rehearsals of every part of the music, which received ample justice in the performance. The result, nevertheless, was disappointment. With many beauties, the work, as a whole, was found to be laboured and heavy; and, though Jenny Lind received the honours due to her illustrious name, and was applauded with enthusiasm in her most brilliant efforts, yet the reception of the piece was not so warm as to encourage its repetition.

In 1857 the only remarkable novelty was the appearance of the celebrated Russian pianist, Rubinstein, who performed a concerto, and several smaller pieces, composed by himself, displaying the powers of a virtuoso of the first class. In 1858, our young and rising pianist Mr. Cusins made his first appearance, performing Sterndale Bennett's concerto in F minor with the warmest applause. Joachim revisited

England this year, and appeared at two of the concerts, where he was received more cordially than ever. Rubinstein, too, reappeared at one of the concerts, performing Weber's *Concert-stück*, and several pieces without the orchestra.

The most remarkable occurrence of the year 1859 was the production of Sterndale Bennett's cantata *The May Queen*, composed for and first performed at the Leeds Festival of the preceding year, of which festival Professor Bennett was the conductor. As this work is now well known to the public, and has taken its place among our English classics, it will suffice to say, that it was admirably performed on this occasion, the principal parts being sung by Madame Clara Novello, Miss Lascelles, Mr. Sims Reeves, and Mr. Weiss, and that it was received with the honour due to a work so beautiful and interesting.

This year Joachim was again in London, and played at two concerts with his usual success. The other solo performers of the season, were the violinists, the brothers Holmes, Mr. Hallé, Madame Schumann, and Miss Arabella Goddard.

In 1860 two distinguished pianists, Herr Lubeck and Herr Ritter appeared, both with success. Herr Becker (joint principal-violin in the orchestra) performed Mendelssohn's concerto; Herr Kömpel performed Spohr's eighth violin concerto; M. Paque a concerto on the violoncello; and Miss Arabella Goddard Dussek's concerto in G minor.

In the end of the year 1860, the Directors, in making the necessary arrangements for the following season, found themselves involved in a serious difficulty. Having, as usual, issued their offer of re-engagement to the members of the orchestra, they received from such of these gentlemen as were also members of the band of the Royal Italian Opera, answers, declining to accept the engagement, and at the same time expressing their regret that they were precluded from doing so by a stipulation inserted for the first time into their engagements at Covent Garden Theatre, according to which their services could be demanded on the Monday evenings throughout the season. This difficulty being found insurmountable, the Directors were constrained, with pain and reluctance, to engage other performers in the room of those of whom they were thus deprived. They numbered above half the orchestra, and among them were many of its oldest and most valued members. The Directors, therefore, considered it due to these gentlemen to express their feelings on the occasion; and accordingly the following letter was addressed to each of them :—

"DEAR SIR,

"I have laid before the Directors of the Philharmonic Society your letter in which, for the reasons therein assigned, you decline to accept the engagement offered to you in the orchestra next season, unless under reservations to which the Directors find it impossible to accede. The number and dates of the concerts were expressly fixed by the last general meeting of the Society, and you are aware that the engagement with the orchestra must necessarily provide for their regular and personal attendance at every concert and rehearsal.

"It is with sincere and deep regret that the Directors find themselves deprived of the assistance of many friends and professional brethren. While they do not complain of your having consulted what you consider as being your own interest in yielding to the influence under which you have acted, they must be permitted to say, that this influence, as you and the musical public cannot but feel, is of an arbitrary and oppressive character, and such as no theatrical manager or musical director has ever, *till now*, thought of exercising. What advantage can be derived by any one from such an interference, is a question into which the Directors will not enter. But in separating from so many valued members of the orchestra, they cannot refrain from reminding you of the relation in which the Philharmonic Society has so long stood with the musical profession of London, and of the circumstances under which this separation has now been forced upon them.

I am, &c.,
G. Hogarth.
Secretary.

"London, *December* 22, 1860."

In filling up the orchestra by means of new engagements the Directors had the good fortune to be very successful. And when the concerts of 1861 commenced it was unanimously admitted by the public that the Philharmonic orchestra had suffered no loss of the qualities by which it had gained its high and European reputation.*

---

* Lists of the orchestra in the Seasons 1860 and 1861, are given in the Appendix.

The concerts of 1861 presented no feature of novelty, in respect either to the music or the performers; but the season, nevertheless, was both brilliant and successful.

The Philharmonic Society being now on the eve of its fiftieth year, the idea of a jubilee celebration naturally suggested itself. The subject was accordingly brought by the Directors before a general meeting called for that purpose, and held on the 20th of May, 1861. Of that meeting the following are the minutes:—

"Mr. M'Murdie said, that he had been requested by the Directors to explain their views upon the subject for which the meeting had been called. He stated, that as next year, 1862, will be the Fiftieth Anniversary of the foundation of the Philharmonic Society, it would probably be deemed fitting, not only by the Subscribers to the concerts, and those specially connected with the Society, but by the public at large, that this period in the annals of an Institution which has had so important an influence on the state of music, should receive some special celebration of the nature of a Jubilee; and that, as such a proceeding would require timely preparation, the Directors thought it might be desirable to bring it immediately under the notice of the Society, with which view they had directed this meeting to be called; and he had been instructed, therefore, to submit to the meeting the following suggestions for their consideration.

"First. That after the eight concerts of next season, an additional concert be given to the subscribers as a compliment, and to the public in general on such terms of admission as may be considered proper; that it be held in Exeter Hall, St. James's Hall, or such other locality as may admit of its being given on a large scale.

"Secondly. That at this concert a selection of the colossal works written expressly for the Society by Beethoven, Spohr, Mendelssohn, and other great composers, be performed.

"Thirdly. That Professor Sterndale Bennett be requested to compose a work, of the class that may be most agreeable to himself, to be performed on this occasion.

"Fourthly. That the Directors be authorised immediately to make the intention of the Society known to the subscribers and the public, by subjoining an announcement to the programmes of the remaining concerts of the season, or in such other way as they may think expedient.

"The meeting having deliberated upon the subject, it was moved by Mr. Goss, and seconded by Mr. Cooke, that the propositions brought forward by the Directors be adopted and carried out, and that the Directors be authorised to take the necessary steps for that purpose. Agreed to unanimously.

"Moved by Mr. Sloper, seconded by Mr. Wright, that the thanks of this meeting be given to the Directors for the prompt and judicious manner in which they have brought forward this matter, and also for the activity and energy with which they have met the difficulties of the present Season. Carried unanimously.

The last event, connected with the Philharmonic Society, which I have to mention, is the lamented death of His Royal Highness the Prince Consort; an event which has suddenly deprived our Sovereign of a beloved Husband, the nation of a great benefactor, and this Society of an illustrious Patron, who has constantly deigned to take a warm interest in its proceedings and its welfare.

APPENDIX.

EXTRACTS OF LETTERS FROM MENDELSSOHN TO STERNDALE BENNETT.

BERLIN, 15th *April*, 1842.

MY DEAR BENNETT,

Mr. Kistner writes me yesterday (dated 12th April), that he sent your box *last week* viâ Hamburgh to you : I hope accordingly that it will reach or has reached you safely. I have made all those alterations in my symphony which I intended (two principal ones in the first movement and some other trifles in all four), but I need not make any remarks about them, or give new directions, it goes all by itself. I hope you will keep your kind promise and superintend the rehearsal as fraternally as possible. You want to know the day or time of my arrival, but you forgot to mention the dates of the Philharmonic Concerts, which are to take place after the 16th May ! I asked you to do so, and beg once more you will do so as soon as possible, because my plans quite depend on it.

You know that I have to conduct the musical festival at Dusseldorf on the 15th and 16th May. I shall not be able to start immediately after those days, but wish to be present for at least two Philharmonic Concerts, and would arrange my stay at Dusseldorf according to your answer.

Pray write by return of post and tell me those dates ; I will then fix the day and time of my arrival as soon as I can. * * *

DUSSELDORF, 13th May, 1842.

MY DEAR FRIEND,

Pray write me word immediately when you receive these lines whether it suits your (the Philharmonic Directors') plans to have any symphony at the 30th May's concert, and my playing at the succeeding, the 13th June? This arrangement I would like *best*, and if you write yes (which implies that you must have received your box and had a trial before my arrival, &c.), I shall be, God willing, in London the 26th or at latest 27th of this month. If you should write no, I would probably arrive a few days later, and change my plans; therefore answer immediately and tell me how it is. I am not sure that I can stay until the 27th of June with you, my time is rather buschränkt: however, I hope to stay as long as I can, and of course should prefer being at two of your concerts to being at one only. I shall write the day of my arrival as soon as I have your answer, which please to direct to this place, with my name only. Excuse the Musikfest-haste. You know it, as also

Your

FELIX M. B.

DUSSELDORF, 18th May, 1842,
In such a haste!

MY DEAR FRIEND,

I have not yet received your answer to my last, but write these lines to beg you to change our plans, and to accept of my assistance at the *two last* Philharmonic Concerts, instead of the sixth and seventh. I am so exhausted with the fatigues of this festival, and have still so much to do before my departure, that I prefer fixing my arrival in London a day or two later, and at all events I should not

APPENDIX. 125

like to be *bound* to be there in so short a time. It would hurry the journey too much, and I do not know whether I should be able to keep my promise and be there in good time and good health : so pray let me have the 13th June instead of the 30th May. * * *

BONN, 23*rd May*, 1842.
MY DEAR BENNETT,

I received here your letter, and although I have written last week from Dusseldorf to beg you to postpone my symphony from the sixth concert to the seventh, I answer your letter once more. My thanks for all kind things you tell me. I shall be happy to conduct the whole concert as the Directors wish me to do, and hope it will not be of great inconvenience that it is to be the 13th of June instead of the 30th May.

BERLIN, 15*th January*, 1844.
MY DEAR BENNETT,

I duly received your kind letter, in which you tell me that you cannot postpone the beginning of the Philharmonic Concerts. Accordingly I tried to ascertain whether I could leave Berlin before Easter, but I am afraid I shall not be able to do so ! My chief occupation is at present the music at the Cathedral here, which seems to interest the King above all things : he wishes to have an Oratorio on Palm Sunday, and some Psalms sung on Easter Sunday, at which my presence would be necessary,—in short, I am afraid I cannot think of leaving Berlin till the day after Easter. The question now is (and I write you therefore these lines in great haste, and beg you will answer them as soon as you possibly can), whether my presence would be still welcome at those Concerts, if I could only come after the two first were over, or whether this circumstance would destroy the whole plan. If I could be of use, although I should arrive only in time for the subsequent Concerts, I beg you will tell me so. I hope that nothing should prevent my being with you at the end of April, and from staying till the Concerts are over. Of course the conditions would be altered, and it should quite remain with your Society to fix them as they like under those altered circumstances.

But if the plan must be given up altogether (which I fear will be the case), perhaps it could be taken up again for another year, when I hope I should be able to leave this place sooner, and when I shall have more liberty to do what I like. For I should be *too* sorry if by this chance I should lose entirely the very great honour which the Society intended to confer upon me by that offer, and I am certain I need not assure you of this any more, for you feel it for me as I do. * * *

BERLIN, *4th March*, 1844.

MY DEAR BENNETT,

Since yesterday I have the certainty of being able to come over to you ; and this morning I received Mr. Watt's official letter. There is superstition for you and for me. I have written to him with how great a pleasure, and how thankfully I accept the honor the Philharmonic Society will do me, and that I shall come—if possible, in time for the 29th of April,—if not, certainly for the last five Concerts ; and that I anticipate such a happy time, such a treat from my stay in England ! The same I must write to you, and thank you ! And do that from my heart ! . . . So pray write me *always* at least two or three days after you receive my letter. I will do the same, and I hope that you will be kind enough to grant me that favour, and perhaps we may thus do some good to your Society. So then to my first questions—

When do you fix the Programmes for each concert? Are there some pieces fixed already and which? Will the Directors allow me a vote or opinion in the composition of their Programmes?

Who are the vocal Artists on which you can depend for the Concerts? Is the choice of their pieces left to them or not? Have you a Chorus at your disposal for every Concert? or for several, or for none?

Have you something new for these Concerts? And do you know of something besides yours? Have the *two Overtures* to Leonore, of Beethoven, that he composed before the one in C, [musical notation] (and the one in E to Fidelio) been performed in England? and has the second Finale to Leonore (manuscript) been ever performed at the Philharmonic? I possess the last, and could perhaps send it over and have an English translation made for it. Should I perhaps bring some new published music, and could we have a trial night of it after my arrival? But even if this were not possible (for which I would be very sorry), should I not bring a copy of the Symphony of Schubert, of that of Gade, and some other good new things that I might get here or at Leipsic, to make our choice from them? I intend also bringing several things of mine, but am not yet quite sure whether I shall finish all I have in my mind; however I hope to.

APPENDIX.

FRANKFORT, *2nd May*, 1844.

As for the Philharmonic Concert of the 13th, I dare say it will be necessary to fix the Programme before my arrival. If that is the case, pray remember what I wrote to you on that subject from Berlin, and let me have at any rate some fine Symphonies and Overtures to conduct for my debût. If the programme (or at least the great instrumental pieces) can be kept open till Thursday, and till we may have talked it over, I should like it best, but if not, once more pray let me have plenty of all sorts of good things for that Concert. I hear many agreeable things of your last Programme, of the crowded and well pleased public, of the manner in which the whole went off. So much the better !

WORKS BY ENGLISH COMPOSERS, WITH THE DATES OF PERFORMANCE.

ATTWOOD, T.

Terzetto, "La Solitudine" . .	24 May, 1819.
Terzetto, "Qual Silenzio" . .	22 May, 1820.
,, ,, .	27 May, 1822.
,, ,, .	7 June, 1824.

BARNETT, J.

Scena, "Ah me, he comes not" (Fair Rosamond) . . .	21 May, 1860.

BENNETT, W. S.

Concerto, P. F., in E. flat . .	11 May, 1835.
(Miss Goddard) . . .	24 May, 1861.
Overture, MS., "The Naiades" .	29 May, 1837.
,, ,, .	8 May, 1843.
,, ,, .	10 June, 1844.
,, ,, .	21 June, 1847.
,, ,, .	1 June, 1857.
,, ,, .	2 July, 1860.
Concerto in F. minor . .	18 June, 1838.
Concerto in F minor, op. 19 .	6 May, 1839.
,,	30 May, 1842.
(Mr. Cusins) . . .	12 April, 1858.
(Miss Goddard) . . .	11 July, 1859.
Overture, "Parisina" . .	4 March, 1839.
,, ,, .	8 June, 1840.
,, ,, .	24 May, 1848.

130   APPENDIX.

Overture, "The Wood Nymphs". 22 April, 1839.
Concerto in C minor . . . 25 April, 1836.
" " . 31 May, 1841.
(Miss Goddard) . . . 9 June, 1856.
Concert-stück . . . . 5 June, 1843.
Caprice . . . . . 20 April, 1846.
(Miss Kate Loder) . . . 22 April, 1850.
"The May Queen" . . . 30 May, 1859.

BISHOP, H. R.
Cantata, "The Seventh Day" . 3 March, 1834.
Cantata, "Paradise" . . . 6 June, 1836.
" " . 16 May, 1853.
Recit. and Air, "Is this the Region" 23 March, 1840.
Recit. and Air, "Fast into the Waves" . . . . } 19 June, 1843.

BURGHERSH, LORD.
Sinfonia, MS. (Presented to the Society) . . . . } 26 May, 1817.

BURROWES.
Finale, MS. (Composed for the Society) . . . . } 15 April, 1816.

CALLCOTT, W. H.
Song, "The Last Man" . . 25 March, 1833.

CRAMER, J. B.
Concerto, (Cramer and Mozart) . 31 May, 1813.
" " . 10 March, 1828.
Quintetto, P. F. &c. . . . 15 May, 1815.
" . 30 April, 1832.
Concerto, MS. . . . . 10 May, 1819.
Quintetto, MS. . . . . 11 March, 1833.

Quintetto, MS. . . . . 3 March, 1834.
Concerto, (No. 5) . . . 23 Feb. 1835.

CROTCH, DR.

Quartetto, "Lo, Star-led Chiefs" (Palestine) . . . . } 31 May, 1813.
,, ,, . 17 April, 1815.
Sinfonia, M.S. . . . . 16 May, 1814.
Sestetto, "Lo, Cherub Bands" (Palestine) . . . . } 13 March, 1815.
Motett, "Methinks I hear" . 19 April, 1819.
Song, "Ye Guardian Saints" (Palestine) . . . . } 17 April, 1837.
,, ,, . 4 June, 1838.
,, ,, . 19 April, 1841.
,, ,, . 3 July, 1843.
Duet, "Such the faint Echo" (Palestine) . . . . } 18 April, 1842.

FIELD, JOHN (of St. Petersburg).

Concerto, P. F. . . . . 27 Feb. 1832.

GOSS, JOHN.

Overture, MS. . . . . 23 April, 1827.

GRIFFIN, G. E.

Quartetto, instrumental . . 28 Feb. 1814.
,, ,, . 24 May, 1819.
Quartetto, P. F., &c. . . 14 April, 1817.

GRIESBACH, J. H.

Overture, MS. . . . . 28 April, 1828.
Overture, "Belshazzar's Feast" . 7 April, 1834.
Overture, "Titania" . . . 15 May, 1848.
Overture, "The Tempest" . . 6 May, 1850.

K 2

APPENDIX.

HATTON, J. L.

    Duet, "Stung by Horror" (Pascal Bruno) . . . . . } 27 May, 1844.

HAYWARD.

    Introduction and Polonaise, violin   23 March, 1840.

HORSLEY, W.

    Motett, "Exaltabo" . . .   7 April, 1834.
    Motett, "Gloria in Excelsis" . .   23 Feb. 1835.

LINDLEY, R.

    Trio, violin, viola, and cello   .   9 March, 1818.
       ,,   ,,   .   19 April, 1819.
    Trio, violin, and two celli . .   5 June, 1820.
    Concertante, two celli obblig. .   23 Feb. 1824.
       ,,   ,,   .   17 April, 1826.
    Concertante, violin, and cello . .   27 April, 1829.

LUCAS, C.

    Overture, ("The Regicide") .   31 May, 1841.
      ,,   ,,   . .   1 June, 1846.
    Sinfonia in B flat, MS. .   30 April, 1855.

MACFARREN, G. A.

    Sinfonia in C sharp, minor . .   9 June, 1845.
    Overture ("Don Quixote") . .   3 May, 1852.
    Overture ("Chevy Chase") . .   11 June, 1855.
    Overture ("Don Carlos") .   14 April, 1856.

NICHOLSON, C.

    Fantasia, flute obblig. . . .   21 April, 1823.
    Concerto flute . . . .   12 June, 1826.
    Concerto flute . . . .   26 May, 1828.
    Fantasia flute   . . . .   28 May, 1832.
    Concerto flute (Mr. Richardson) .   16 May, 1842.

APPENDIX.

NOVELLO, V.

    "Rosalba," dramatic cantata   17 March, 1834.

POTTER, C.

    Overture . . . . . 11 March, 1816.
    Adagio and characteristic rondo, P. F. . . . . . } 3 May, 1830.
    Sinfonia, MS. . . . . 8 June, 1835.
    Sinfonia in D . . . . 21 March, 1836.
        ,,   22 April, 1850.
    Overture ("Cymbeline") . . 3 April, 1837.
        ,,   ,,   12 May, 1851.
    Overture ("Antony and Cleopatra") 12 May, 1856.

SMART, H.

    Scene from "As you like it," 4 voices and chorus . . . } 8 July, 1844.

THOMAS, JOHN.

    Concerto in E flat, harp . . 3 May, 1852.

WESLEY, S.

    Motett, MS. "Father of Light" . 29 April, 1816.

VOCAL PERFORMERS WHO HAVE APPEARED AT THE CONCERTS.

FEMALE PERFORMERS.

Ashe, Mrs.
Ashe, Miss H.
Andrews, Miss
Alboni, Madame.
Aïrtôt, Mademoiselle.
Albertazzi, Madame.

Bolton, Miss.
Bacon, Miss.
Bishop, Mrs. (late Miss Riviere).
Bassano, Miss.
Birch, Miss.
Bruce, Miss.
Balfe, Madame.
Babbnigg, Mademoiselle.
Brambilla, Signora.
Blasis, Mademoiselle.
Begnis, Madame de.
Bildstein, Mademoiselle.
Bertrand, Mademoiselle.
Biscacciante, Madame.
Borchart, Madame.
Bertucat, Mademoiselle.

Corri, Miss.
Carew, Miss.
Childe, Miss (Mrs. E. Seguin).
Cawse, Miss H.
Cramer, Miss.
Chambers, Miss.
Csillag, Mademoiselle.
Camporese, Madame.
Catalani, Madame.
Caradori Allan, Madame.
Cornega, Madame.
Canzi, Signora.
Colleoni Corti, Madame.
Caton, Madame.
Castellan, Madame.
Corbari, Mademoiselle.
Charton, Mademoiselle.

Dickons, Mrs.
Dolby, Miss (Mad. Sainton).
Duval, Miss.
De Lihu, Mademoiselles.
Damoreau, Madame Cinti.
Devrient, Madame Schrœder.

APPENDIX. 135

Enderssohn, Mrs.
Eckerlin, Madame.

Flower, Miss.
Fodor, Madame.
Falconi, Mademoiselle.
Fincklor, Madame.

Goodall, Miss.
Grisi, Madame.
Griglietti, Miss.
Gras, Madame Dorus.
Guerrabella, Madame.

Hughes, Miss.
Hawes, Miss M. B.
Hayes, Miss C.
Hennelle, Madame.

Inverarity, Miss.

Kemble, Miss A.
Knyvett, Mrs. W.
Kearns, Miss.
Klinger, Madame.
Knispel, Madame.
Krall, Mademoiselle.

Lacy, Madame Bianchi.
Lucombe, Miss.
Lockey, Mrs. (Miss M. Williams).
Lascelles, Miss.
Lalande, Madame.

Lœwe, Mademoiselle.
Lind, Madame Goldschmidt.

Masson, Miss.
Mori, Miss.
Marshall, Miss.
Malibran, Madame.
Meric, Madame de.
Moralt, Madame.
Mamo, Madame Borghi.
Marinoni, Signora.
Maillard, Madame.
Michael, Mademoiselle.
Meyer, Mademoiselle.
Meerti, Mademoiselle.

Novello, Madame Clara.
Novello, Miss S.
Noble, Mrs.
Naldi, Mademoiselle.
Nau, Mademoiselle.
Nottes, Madame.
Ney, Mademoiselle Jenny.

Paton, Miss (Mrs. Wood).
Postans, Miss (Mrs. A. Shaw).
Poole, Miss.
Pyne, Miss L.
Pyne, Miss S.
Puzzi, Madame.
Placci, Mademoiselle.
Persiani, Madame.
Pacini, Mademoiselle.
Parepa, Mademoiselle.

Pasta, Madame.

Rainforth, Miss.
Rovedino, Miss.
Rivieri, Madame de.
Rummel, Mademoiselle.
Rieder, Madame.
Rudersdorff, Madame.

Salmon, Mrs.
Stephens, Miss.
Shirreff, Miss.
Steele, Miss.
Stabbach, Miss.
Sontag, Mademoiselle.
Schutz, Madame.
Stockhausen, Madame.
Sherrington, Madame.
Schrickel, Mademoiselle.
Schloss, Mademoiselle.
Specchi, Mademoiselle.

Tree, Miss M.
Toulmin, Mrs.
Thornton, Miss.
Thomson, Miss A.
Thillon, Madame.
Treffz, Mademoiselle de.

Vaughan, Mrs.
Vestris, Madame.
Vigo, Madame.
Villowen, Madame.
Vera, Mademoiselle.
Viardot, Madame.

Williams, Miss A.
Woodyatt, Miss.
Weiss, Mrs.
Wranizki, Madame.
Westerstrand, Madame.

MALE PERFORMERS.

Allen.
Angrisani.

Braham.
Bradley.
Bellamy.
Bennett.
Bradbury.
Balfe.
Benson.
Bodda.
Beale.
Begrez.
Bianchi.
Begnis, de.
Brizzi.
Belletti.
Belart.
Bordogni.

Corri, P. A.
Cooke, T.
Chapman.
Calkin.
Cooper, W.
Coles.
Crivelli.
Curioni.
Cartagenova.
Catoni.

Costa.
Coletti.

Delle Sedie.
Donzelli.

Evans.
Elliot.
Eicke.

Formes.

Goss.
Garcia.
Giubilei.
Gatti.
Gardoni.

Hawes.
Hobbs.
Horncastle.
Hawkins.
Hatton, J. L.
Haitzinger.

Ivanoff.

Kellner.
Knyvett, W.
Kroff.

Lacy.
Leete.
Lawler.
Leonard.
Lockey.
Ledesma.
Levasseur.
Lablache.
Lablache, F.

Magrath.
Marshall.
Machin.
Manvers.
Mayer.
Marzocchi.
Mario.
Mariani.

Novello, A.
Nelson.
Naldi.

Oberhoffer.

Phillips, H.
Parry.
Pearsall.
Pellegrini.
Ponchard.

Placci.	Smith, C.	Taylor, E.
Pischek.	Sale.	Tennant.
	Seguin, E.	Tamburini.
Reeves, S.	Stretton.	
Rafter.	Smith, Montem.	Vaughan.
Rosquellas.	Santley.	Vrugh.
Reyes.	Smithson.	
Rovedino.	Sapio.	Welch, T.
Rosner.	Staudigl.	Whitworth.
Rubini.	Stockhausen.	Weiss.
Revial.	Salvi.	Wartel.
Reichardt.	Santini.	Winter.
Remorini.		
Ronconi.	Terrail.	Zuchelli.

APPENDIX.

MEMBERS, ASSOCIATES, AND FEMALE ASSOCIATES: SEASON 1862.

MEMBERS.

*Those marked thus * are Directors for the year* 1862.

*Mr. Anderson, G. F.
Prof. W. S. Bennett
Messrs. Bennett, James.
,, Benson, G.
,, Blagrove, H.
,, Calkin, James.
,, Calkin, Joseph T.
,, Card, W.
,, Chatterton, J. Balsir.
,, Clinton, J.
,, Cooke, H. A. M.
,, *Cusins, W. G.
,, Dorrell, W.
,, *Ferrari, A.
,, Forbes, G.
,, Goss, J.
,, Griesbach, J. Henry.
,, Griffin, G. E.
,, Holmes, W. H.
,, Jewson, F. B.

Messrs. Lucas, C.
,, *M'Murdie, J., M. B.
,, Neate, C.
,, Osborne, G. A.
,, Potter, C.
,, Richards, Brinley.
,, Sainton, P.
,, Schulz, E.
,, Sloper, Lindsay.
,, Stephens, C. E.
Sir G. Smart.
Messrs. Thomas, J.
,, Thomas, Harold.
,, *Turle, J.
,, Walmisley, T. F.
,, Westrop, H.
,, *Williams, Joseph.
,, Wright, T. H.
,, *Wilson, M. C.

APPENDIX.

ASSOCIATES.

Messrs. Aguilar, E.
" Banister, H. C.
" Banister, Jos.
" Barnett, R.
" Berger, Francesco.
" Bodda, F.
" Burrowes, J. F.
" Calkin, J. B.
" Callcott, W. H.
" Cooper, G.
" Cooper, J. T.
" Gardner, C., jun.
" Gear, H.
" Gilbert, A.
" Gledhill, J.
" Graves, H.

Messrs. Henshaw, T. W.
" Hopkins, E. J.
" Horsley, C. E.
" King, G. Manton.
" Lablache, F.
" Layland.
" Lazarus, H.
" Lockey, C.
" Macfarren, W. C.
" Pye, K., Mus. Bac.
" Redfearn, W.
" Sale, G.
" Stephens, S. J.
" Trust, H. J.
" Wallace, W. Vincent
" Webb, W. H.

FEMALE ASSOCIATES.

Allan, Madame Caradori.
Andrews, Mrs. J. H.
Bartholomew, Mrs. Mounsey.
Birch, Miss.
Calkin, Miss.
Cazaly, Miss S.
Cooper, Mrs.
Dolby, Madame Sainton.
Ferrari, Madame.
Jewson, Mrs. F. B.

Macirone, Miss.
Masson, Miss.
Mounsey, Miss E.
Phillips, Mrs. H.
Reinagle, Mrs.
Sampson, Mrs.
Seguin, Mrs. W. H.
Steele, Miss.
Thompson, Mrs.
Wilson, Miss Annette.

HONORARY MEMBERS.

M. Auber.
M. Berlioz.
M. Gadé.
M. Halévy.
Herr Hauptmann.
M. Hiller.
M. Joachim.
Herr Liszt.
Herr Marschner.

Herr Meyerbeer.
M. Moscheles.
M. Rietz.
Signor Rossini.
M. Rubinstein.
M. Thalberg.
M. Verhulst.
Herr Wagner.

LIST OF THE ORCHESTRA: SEASONS 1860—61.

1860.

FIRST VIOLINS.

Mr. H. Blagrove, } Princip.
M. Becker,
Messrs. J. Banister.
,, M. Bezeth.
,, J. T. Carrodus.
,, R. Clementi.
,, G. A. Griesbach.
,, H. Hill.
,, L. Ries.
,, J. W. Thirlwall.
,, A. Tolbecque.
,, I. B. Zerbini.

SECOND VIOLINS.

Messrs. W. Watson (Prin.)
,, C. D. Betts.
,, T. Browne.
,, J. J. Calkin.
,, H. Griesbach.
,, J. Jay.
,, J. M. Marshall.
,, J. Newsham.
,, E. Nickel.

Messrs. E. Payton.
,, E. Perry.
,, A. Streather.

VIOLAS.

Messrs. Webbe (Principal).
,, W. J. Glanville.
,, R. Hann.
,, W. Thomas.
,, J. Thompson.
,, H. J. Trust.
,, J. Weslake.
,, T. Westrop.

VIOLONCELLOS.

Messrs. C. Lucas (Principal).
,, W. H. Aylward.
,, G. Calkin.
,, T. Guest.
,, T. W. Hancock.
,, G. Paque.
,, W. F. Reed.
,, L. N. Schroeder.

APPENDIX. 143

DOUBLE BASSES.

Messrs. J. Howell (Principal).
,, W. J. Castell.
,, T. Edgar.
,, G. Flower.
,, G. L. Mount.
,, F. S. Pratten.
,, J. Reynolds.
,, C. Severn.

FLUTES.

Messrs. R. S. Pratten.
,, E. Card.

OBOES.

Messrs. A. Nicholson.
,, H. Malsch.

CLARINETS.

Messrs. J. Williams.
,, H. Lazarus.

BASSOONS.

Messrs. J. G. Waetzig.
,, A. W. Chisholm.

HORNS.

Messrs. C. Harper.
,, J. Catchpole.
,, A. Kielbach.
,, J. W. Standen.

TRUMPETS.

Messrs. C. Zeiss.
,, J. B. Irwin.

TROMBONES.

Messrs. F. Cioffi.
,, A. F. Germann.
,, Webster.

DRUMS.

Mr. T. P. Chipp.

1861.

FIRST VIOLINS.

Mr. H. Blagrove, } Princip
M. Becker,

Messrs. J. Banister.
,, M. Bezeth.
,, V. Buziau.
,, R. Clementi.
,, V. Collins.
,, J. Day.

Messrs. G. A. Griesbach.
,, J. Jacquin.
,, A. Kettenus.
,, J. W. Rendle.

SECOND VIOLINS.

Messrs. E. Payton (Prin.)
,, C. D. Betts.
,, G. Boosé.

Messrs. J. J. Calkin.
„ J. W. Gunniss.
„ J. Jay.
„ W. A. Loades.
„ J. C. Nickel.
„ E. Perry.
„ F. Schoenig.
„ H. Wheatley.
„ Van Hedinghem.

VIOLAS.

Messrs. R. Blagrove (Prinpl.).
„ C. Baetens.
„ E. Boileau.
„ C. Colchester.
„ H. Lutgen.
„ H. Tolhurst.
„ W. Thomas.
„ J. Weslake.

VIOLONCELLOS.

Messrs. W. Pettit (Prinpl.).
„ A. Pezze.
„ H. D. Daubert.
„ H. W. Goodban.
„ S. Smith.
„ L. Schroeder.
„ E. Vieuxtemps.
„ H. Wohlers.

DOUBLE BASSES.

Messrs. A. Rowland (Prinpl.).
„ W. Blakeston.
„ T. Edgar.
„ U. Gilardoni.

Messrs. W. Griffiths.
„ B. Pickaert.
„ J. Waud.
„ C. White.

FLUTES.

Messrs. O. Svindsen.
„ E. Card.

OBOES.

Messrs. A. Lavigne.
„ H. Malsch.

CLARINETS.

Messrs. Jos. Williams.
„ W. Pollard.

BASSOONS.

Messrs. J. G. Waetzig
„ A. Chisholm.

HORNS.

Messrs. H. Steglich.
„ W. Handley.
„ R. Keevil.
„ R. Waterson.

TRUMPETS.

Messrs. C. Zeiss.
„ R. J. Ward.

TROMBONES.

Messrs. W. Webster.
„ A. F. Germann.
„ W. B. Healey.

DRUMS.

Mr. C. J. Thompson.

APPENDIX. 145

LIST OF MEMBERS WHO HAVE SERVED THE OFFICE OF DIRECTORS.

———◆———

ANDERSON, G. F.
Attwood, T.
Ayrton, W.

Braham, J.
Bishop, H. R.
Bennett, W. S.
Burrowes, J. F.
Blagrove, H.
Benedict, J.

Clementi, M.
Corri, P. A.
Cramer, J. B.
Cramer, F.
Calkin, Jas.
Calkin, Jos.
Card, W.
Chatterton, J. B.
Crotch, Dr.
Clinton, J.
Cooke, T.
Cusins, W. G.

Dizi.
Dance.

Elliot, Jas.

Ferrari.

Griffin, G. E.
Griesbach, J. H.

Horsley, W.
Holmes, W. H.
Howell, J.

Jewson, F. B.

Kalkbrenner.
Kramer.
Kiesewetter.

Latour.
Lucas, C.
Lindley, R.
Loder, J.

Meyer, C.
M'Murdie, J.
Moralt.
Mountain.
Moscheles.
Mori, N.

Neate, C.
Naldi.

Potter, sen.
Potter, C.

Ries, F.

Smart, Sir G.
Smart, H., sen.
Sherrington.
Shield.
Spagnoletti.
Sainton, P.
Schulz, E.
Stephens, C. E.
Salomon.

Turle, J.

Viotti.

Weichsell.
Wright, T. H.
Willman, T.
Wilson, M. C.
Williams, J.
Welch, T.
Webbe, S.
Wesley, S.

L

PATRONS OF THE PHILHARMONIC SOCIETY.

From 1813 to 1819, HIS ROYAL HIGHNESS THE PRINCE REGENT.
From 1820 to 1830, KING GEORGE THE FOURTH.
From 1831 to 1837, KING WILLIAM THE FOURTH and QUEEN ADELAIDE.
From 1837 to the present time, QUEEN VICTORIA.
In 1851 the names of HIS ROYAL HIGHNESS THE PRINCE CONSORT and HER ROYAL HIGHNESS THE DUCHESS OF KENT were added.

TREASURERS.

In 1813 and 1814, W. Ayrton.
In 1815, W. Dance.
In 1816 and 1817, M. Clementi.
In 1818 and 1819, R. H. Potter.
In 1820, T. Attwood.
From 1821 to 1832, W. Dance.
In 1833, 1834, 1835, W. Sherrington.
In 1836, 1837, and 1838, W. Dance.
Since 1839, G. F. Anderson.

For EU product safety concerns, contact us at Calle de José Abascal, 56–1º,
28003 Madrid, Spain or eugpsr@cambridge.org.

www.ingramcontent.com/pod-product-compliance
Ingram Content Group UK Ltd.
Pitfield, Milton Keynes, MK11 3LW, UK
UKHW041418180426
11947UKWH00007B/201